100 GREATEST WOMEN

DRAGON'S WORLD

CHILDREN'S BOOKS

DRAGON'S WORLD

CHILDREN'S BOOKS

First published in Great Britain in 1995
by Dragon's World Limited
Reprinted 1998.

Dragon's World Limited
London House
Great Eastern Wharf
Parkgate Road
London SW11 4NQ

Text: Angela Royston
Editor: Kyla Barber
Copy Editor: Claire Watts
Designer: Mel Raymond
Design Assistants: Karen Ferguson
                            Victoria Furbisher
Picture Research: Josine Meijer
Art Director: John Strange
Editorial Director: Pippa Rubinstein

The catalogue record for this book
is available from the British Library.

ISBN 1 85028 307 9

Printed in Italy

Contents

Introduction

It is only in the last hundred years that women have begun to be seen as equal to men. Throughout much of history, women have played a secondary role to men. Think up a list of great people in almost any area – rulers, explorers, doctors, inventors – and the list will be made up largely of men. Women who do appear on such a list usually had to struggle for their success, against obstacles presented not just by the society they lived in, but often by their families, too.

One of the major obstacles to women in the past was their lack of education. While boys were sent to school so that they could learn to take their place in the world, women were expected to aim at making a good marriage, learning to take care of a house and having children. In the eighteenth century, a few women, such as Mary Wollstonecraft, began to speak out against this injustice, arguing that women needed to be educated so that they could free themselves from the need to marry for money.

Inequality was not just confined to matters of education. Even at a time when the monarch of one of the world's empires was a woman, Queen Victoria, women were not thought clever enough to have the vote, and certainly not clever enough to stand for parliament. It was towards the end of Victoria's reign that women from many countries, such as Jeanette Rankin and Emmeline Pankhurst, joined the suffragette movement, campaigning for equal rights for women, including the right to vote.

As well as fighting for themselves, women have tried to change the world for others, too. Florence Nightingale set out for the Crimea to nurse wounded soldiers and ended up changing the way hospitals were run the world over. Former slaves Sojourner Truth and Harriet Tubman fought for the abolition of the terrible injustice of slavery. Eleanor Roosevelt helped to forge the Universal Declaration of Human Rights, and Eglantyne Jebb was among those who put it into practice all over the world.

In this book, you can read not just about the determined women who finally won equal rights, and those who helped to change the world in some way, but about many other courageous and determined women who excelled in all kinds of fields. From rulers and explorers to writers and musicians, women feature among the greatest on any list. Even so, the battle for equality between men and women is still not won, and many women in the world still have to fight for the right to be recognized as equal to men.

Florence Nightingale (top left)
Elizabeth I of England (top centre)
Shikibu Murasaki (bottom left)
Anna Pavlova (right)
Margaret Mead (below)

Elizabeth Fry
(1780-1845)

Elizabeth Fry was unusual. Most people tried to avoid prison, but she went inside to see for herself how women and children lived there. She was so appalled she decided to try to change things.

Elizabeth was born in Norfolk and her family were Quakers. In 1813, she heard about the conditions in Newgate Prison and, with a group of other Quakers, visited the most terrible prison in England. Women and children crowded around Elizabeth. She saw how they gambled, drank and stole from each other because they had nothing else to do. Elizabeth returned to Newgate regularly. She set up a school for the children in an empty cell. She brought the women sewing work and paid them for it.

Elizabeth formed a prisoners' aid society and tried to persuade Parliament to change the prisons. The authorities listened to her; they could see that her methods worked. Prisons in Europe as well as Britain began to change.

▲ In 1780, the year of Elizabeth's birth, there was a riot at Newgate Prison. The buildings and furniture were burned and 300 prisoners were released.

The Quakers are a Christian group who believe strongly in peace and in helping other people. Even as a child, Elizabeth was used to visiting sick people and teaching poor children.

Florence Nightingale
(1820-1910)

Although Florence Nightingale visited the poor and sick with her mother, her parents would not allow her to become a nurse. Nursing was not considered a suitable job for a respectable woman in those days. Nurses were untrained and often drunk. Instead, Florence read everything she could about hospitals and public health. She persuaded her parents to let her spend three months at a German school for nurses.

In 1853, the Crimean War broke out. When Florence heard that wounded British soldiers were dying in terrible conditions, she gathered a group of nurses together and sailed to the Crimea and the battlefront. She found that the army hospital was filthy and overrun with rats. The women cleaned up the hospital and dressed the soldiers' wounds. The death rate among wounded soldiers fell from about fifty per cent to almost nothing. The doctors and male orderlies resented Florence and her nurses, but the wounded soldiers loved them.

When news of Florence's achievements reached Britain, she became a national heroine. Florence set up a school of nursing at St Thomas' Hospital in London, and used her influence to improve the way hospitals were run. Nursing became a respectable profession, and in 1907, Florence received the Order of Merit, one of Britain's highest awards.

Florence was not the only British nurse to go to the Crimea. Mary Seacole, whose mother was Jamaican and father Scottish, volunteered to go too, but was turned down because she was black. She went anyway and opened the British Hotel with a hospital on the upper floor. She, too, saved many lives.

▼ Florence Nightingale became known as 'The Lady with the Lamp' as a result of her night-time rounds in the military hospital.

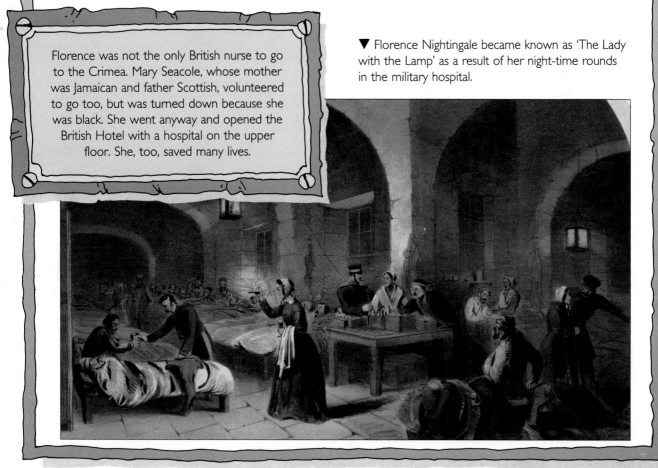

Clara Barton
(1821-1912)

Clara Barton was a timid child, but as an adult, she spoke out to help wounded soldiers and the victims of disasters, and persuaded the United States to join the International Red Cross.

Clara was born in Massachusetts and was always concerned about people less well off than herself. She set up one of the first free schools for the public in New Jersey, but resigned when a man was put in charge over her.

In 1861, the American Civil War broke out. Clara went to the battlefields to see what she could do to help. She loaded up a team of mules with food, water and medical supplies which she distributed to wounded soldiers. Several times, she was nearly killed herself. In 1869, she went to Europe to rest, but instead she volunteered to help in the war between France and Prussia. She saw the newly founded Red Cross in action and was determined that the United States should join it. When she returned home in 1874, she campaigned long and hard to set up an American Red Cross. She argued that it should help not just wounded soldiers, but victims of floods, famine and other disasters as well. She succeeded, and in 1881, she became the first president of the American Red Cross.

▲ When this portrait of a nurse was painted in the early twentieth century, the Red Cross was famous all over the world for its work helping wounded soldiers and victims of natural disasters.

The International Red Cross was started by Henri Dunant in 1864. In 1859, he had stumbled upon a battle between the French and Austrians and had been appalled to see how little was done to help wounded soldiers. The Red Cross cares for all soldiers whatever their nationality or creed.

▶ This poster was produced during World War I to encourage people to give money to the Red Cross. The victims of the war in Europe look across the ocean to the United States for help.

THEY ARE LOOKING TO US FOR HELP
ARE YOU ONE OF US?
ADD YOUR BIT TO THE RED CROSS WAR FUND

Eglantyne Jebb
(1876-1928)

Everyone has heard of the Save the Children Fund, the huge charity which puts the needs of children first. Few people, however, have heard of Eglantyne Jebb, the remarkable woman who started it.

Eglantyne grew up in Shropshire in England. She was an energetic tomboy who nevertheless loved reading. Universities had just opened their doors to women, and Eglantyne seized the chance to study at Oxford. She trained as a teacher and then worked for the Charity Organisation Society. In 1913, she was sent to Macedonia to distribute money to refugees who had lost their homes in the Balkan Wars. She realized then that handing out money to refugees wasn't enough. The people needed to be resettled on the land.

At the end of World War I, millions of families in Europe were starving. Eglantyne started a Fight the Famine Council and a separate fund called Save the Children. At first, people said she was a traitor to raise money for the enemy, but Eglantyne argued that the needs of the children must come first. Money poured into the fund. It was used to set up hospitals, homes and schools.

Eglantyne set up very clear aims and rules for the fund, which are still followed today. They include looking after children, whatever their race, nationality or creed, and helping families care for themselves.

Eglantyne Jebb believed passionately in the need to look after children. 'Every generation of children offers mankind anew the possibility of rebuilding his ruin of a world,' she said. In 1923, she wrote a declaration setting out the rights of children. It was later adopted by the United Nations.

▼ In 1921 a famine in Russia threatened millions of people, including many children, with starvation. The Save the Children Fund was able to help.

Helen Keller
(1880-1968)

When Helen Keller was only nineteen months old, she became ill with scarlet fever. It left her blind and deaf. Her only contact with the world was through her sense of touch, but with the dedicated teaching of one person, Helen learned to read and to speak. She used her abilities to help other deaf and blind people.

The Kellers lived in Alabama in the south of the United States. They had to travel to Boston in New England to get help for the young Helen. Annie Sullivan had just graduated as a teacher for deaf people when she came to live with Helen in 1887. Annie tapped out the names of things on Helen's hand. The taps meant nothing to Helen, who had never been able to communicate with other people in any way. Then one day, Helen realized that when Annie put her hand under water she was tapping the word 'water'. Helen made rapid progress after that. By placing Helen's hand over her lips and throat as she spoke, Annie taught her to recognize words by feeling the vibrations. Helen learned Braille, too, but Annie continued to tap out words on her hand. She helped Helen study at school and university by tapping out the lectures. Helen wrote books and articles about her experiences. She learned to talk and toured all over the United States and Europe giving lectures and raising money to help deaf and blind people.

To learn to speak, Helen Keller had to imitate the vibrations and lip movements she felt other people making. At first, no one could understand her, but she gradually learned to turn the squeaks and grunts she produced into a recognizable voice.

▶ Helen Keller went on a lecture tour across the United States to raise money for the American Foundation for the Blind. She and Annie Sullivan raised $2 million on the tour.

Mother Theresa of Calcutta
(born 1910)

The people who know Mother Theresa best are the poor, blind, sick and abandoned people of Calcutta. She, and the order of nuns she has founded, provide them with schools, homes, medicines and, most of all, care.

Mother Theresa was born in Albania, and christened Agnes Gonxha Bojaxhiu. While she was still at school, she knew that she wanted to work among the poor people in India. When she was only 19, she joined a convent in Calcutta as a teacher and became 'Sister Theresa'. She taught for twenty years, but became more and more distressed by the number of very poor people she saw.

She decided to live and work among them. She set up a school for slum children and took food and medicines to the needy. She opened a refuge for dying people and abandoned babies. She started a new order of nuns, dedicated to helping the poor and sick. News of her work gradually spread, not only in Calcutta but to the rest of the world. She was awarded the Nobel Peace Prize for her work with poor, sick and oppressed people.

▲ Mother Theresa's own work with the poor has been in India, but her order of nuns, the Missionaries of Charity, work with the poor, sick and needy in countries all over the world.

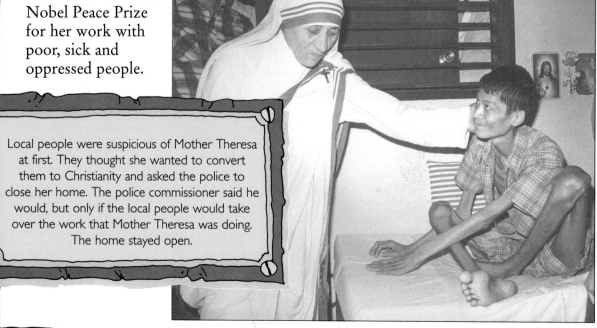

Local people were suspicious of Mother Theresa at first. They thought she wanted to convert them to Christianity and asked the police to close her home. The police commissioner said he would, but only if the local people would take over the work that Mother Theresa was doing. The home stayed open.

Cicely Saunders
(born 1918)

Cicely Saunders has spent her life helping people face death. She opened the first hospice as a place where people who were incurably ill could die in peace and dignity. Today, there are hospices all over the world.

Cicely was so shy when she was a child she would miss her mid-morning drink rather than sit with her noisy classmates. When she grew up, she became a nurse during World War II, and then, when she injured her back, she had to give up nursing and become a hospital social worker instead. In 1947, one of the patients she met was David Tasma, a Polish Jew who was dying. Cicely was a committed Christian, and she and David spent many hours discussing death and how dying people are looked after. They became close friends, and Cicely realized that her conversations with David could help other people. She talked to people who

were dying, sat by their beds, waited and prayed. But she knew that for many people the noise and bustle of hospital were not the best surroundings for them. She campaigned to raise money, and in 1967, she opened St Christopher's Hospice in London. This was a quiet place where people could find care and understanding during their last days.

In the past, death was part of everyday life. Although today you will hear plenty of talk about sex, family problems and money, most people do not like to talk openly about death. This makes it more difficult for people who know they are dying to accept what is happening to them.

◀ The prospect of death has always been difficult to cope with. The work of Cicely Saunders has helped many feel more comfortable in the last days of their lives.

Sue Ryder
(born 1923)

Sue Ryder (Lady Ryder of Warsaw) has devoted her life to helping people who are disabled, sick or suffering.

She was born in Yorkshire and started training as a nurse at the beginning of World War II, then joined a special operations unit which was responsible for co-ordinating the activities of the Resistance in Nazi-occupied Europe. Sue witnessed how much people had suffered during the war. Millions died, many lost their homes, were sick and had no money. After the war, she became involved in relief work in Poland, where she was attached to a medical team. In 1952-3, she returned to Britain, registered the Sue Ryder Foundation as a charity and opened a home in Suffolk for people who had survived the horrors of concentration camps. She soon extended her home to include people of all nationalities who were physically or mentally disabled.

▲ Sue Ryder travels extensively, particularly in central and southern Europe and the developing world, and wherever she finds desperate need she does her utmost to relieve the suffering.

The Sue Ryder Foundation was set up to seek out and face up to human suffering and to do something about it. It tries to help those in need and give affection to those who are unloved, whatever their age, race or creed.

◀ Today there are Mobile Medical Teams and over eighty Sue Ryder homes in different parts of the world. Part of the funding comes from a network of shops. People donate goods which are sold to raise money for the Sue Ryder Foundation.

Anne Frank
(1929-1945)

Anne Frank died when she was just a teenager, and became famous because her fascinating diaries survived her. Anne was Jewish and was born in Germany. When she was 4 years old, the Nazis came to power in Germany. The Nazis hated Jews. They beat them up in the street and took their businesses from them. Anne Frank's parents fled with Anne and her sister to Holland. But in 1940, the Nazis invaded Holland. The Franks were in great danger. They could be sent to brutal work camps or to concentration camps. It was too late to leave, so they decided to hide. They made a secret annexe at the top of Mr Frank's old warehouse and moved in with four other Jewish friends.

For two years, they never went out. Dutch friends smuggled in food for them, but life was very boring. In March 1944, Anne started to write a diary. She hoped to be a writer when she grew up, but in October 1944, someone betrayed the secret annexe to the police. The Franks were arrested and sent to concentration camps in Germany. Only Anne's father was still alive at the end of the war. His Dutch friend had found Anne's diaries and kept them safe.

▲ This photograph of Anne Frank was taken in 1940, at school in Holland before the Nazis took over. Soon she would be in hiding and writing her diary.

Dit is een foto, zoals ik me zou wensen, altijd zo te zijn. Dan had ik nog wel een kans om naar Holywood te komen.

Anne Frank. 10 Oct. 1942

(translation)
"This is a photo as I would wish myself to look all the time. Then I would maybe have a chance to come to Hollywood."
Anne Frank, 10 Oct. 1942

▲ This photograph was found with Anne's diary. When her diary was finally published, in 1947, thousands of copies were sold all over the world.

The Franks and their friends had to keep very quiet in the annexe. They never wore shoes and they had to burn all their rubbish. They often got on each other's nerves and they dreamed of what they would do when they could live normally again.

Mary Wollstonecraft
(1759-1797)

Mary Wollstonecraft believed men and women to be equal, and that they should have the same right to education, work and the vote. Few would argue with her today, but 200 years ago, most people were outraged by these ideas.

Mary's brother was trained to be a lawyer, but she was expected only to find a husband. She was determined to earn her own money. In 1782, she rented a house in Newington Green, then a village near London, and opened a school. The school was not successful, but Mary met a group of people who shared many of her ideas. In 1787, she wrote *Thoughts on the Education of Daughters*. It argued that women needed to be educated so that

▲ Mary Wollstonecraft's feminist ideas were very much ahead of their time.

they did not have to rely on men for money. Mary earned enough from writing to keep herself. But she longed to find a man who would love her as an equal. In 1797 she married William Godwin and that year gave birth to a daughter, but died of fever a few days later.

Mary's daughter was also called Mary. When she grew up, she married the poet Shelley and wrote the novel *Frankenstein*. She got the idea when on holiday with Shelley and Byron. Bryon suggested they should each write a ghost story.

◄ Mary Shelley's *Frankenstein: or The Modern Prometheus*, has been made into a number of famous films.

Sojourner Truth
(1777-1883)

Sojourner Truth was born into slavery. When she was freed, she travelled across the United States, preaching about freedom and equality for black people and women. She was born on a farm in New York state and named Isabella. She was sold many times and married to another slave before she received her freedom in 1826. She became a servant in the houses of wealthy New Yorkers. Her children were still slaves and she longed to see them freed too.

In 1843, she set out as a travelling preacher. She took the name Sojourner Truth because she didn't want to have a slave's name. She preached that all slaves should be freed and joined a group of abolitionists who believed that women too were unjustly treated.

When slavery was at last abolished, she stayed in Washington to help freed slaves start a new life and to protest against the racial discrimination that tried to keep them as badly off as before.

▲ Since Sojourner Truth could neither read nor write, she dictated her life story to a friend, so that people would know what it was like to be a slave.

▼ Slaves being sold. Sojourner Truth met President Abraham Lincoln to encourage him to fight against the southern slave states and stop the trade.

Many people disagreed with Sojourner Truth. One minister said that if God had intended women to be equal to men he would have given a sign through Jesus Christ. Sojourner replied that Christ was born of God and a woman, and so men had nothing to do with Him.

Harriet Beecher Stowe
(1811-1896)

When Harriet Beecher Stowe was born, people in the southern states of the USA still used slaves to work for them. In 1852, Harriet's novel *Uncle Tom's Cabin* helped to persuade thousands of people that slavery should be abolished.

Harriet was born and grew up in Connecticut. In 1832, she went to Cincinnati to teach at her sister Catherine's college. Here, on the northern bank of the Ohio River, she was well aware of the horrors of slavery, as many runaway slaves were caught trying to cross the river to freedom. Slavery was not allowed in the northern states, and runaways became free people there. In 1850, however, the government passed an Act which said that northerners must return runaway slaves or become criminals themselves. Harriet, like many other 'abolitionists', was outraged. She had already written many articles and stories. She wrote *Uncle Tom's Cabin* as a serial in a magazine. The heroic story of a runaway slave jumping from ice floe to ice floe across the Ohio River, gripped the imagination of its readers. It sold thousands of copies. Today, its hero, Tom, is criticized for not fighting his white masters but the story deeply affected people at the time.

▼ These slaves are planting sweet potatoes on a large plantation in South Carolina. For most of the slaves there was little hope of freedom.

Between 1861 and 1865, the American Civil War was fought between the Unionists in the North who wanted to abolish slavery and the Confederates in the South who wanted to keep their slaves. The Unionists won, and slavery was abolished.

Susan Anthony
(1820-1906)

Susan Anthony was born in Massachusetts and trained as a teacher. In 1849, she left teaching to manage the family farm. Her family were Quakers and Susan spoke out against the injustice of slavery and the evils of drunkenness. In 1848, she went to the first convention on women's rights.

Four years later, she was outraged when, as a woman, she was not allowed to speak at a rally against alcohol. Instead she formed a temperance society just for women. From then on, while she continued to campaign against slavery, she also argued for equal rights for women. She edited a journal called *Revolution* which demanded that women should have the same rights as men in education, voting and employment. When the journal ran out of money, she toured the country giving lectures to raise funds for it.

In 1872, she and eleven other women tried to vote in the presidential election. Susan cast a vote and was arrested. She was convicted and fined, but the case was then dropped, even though she refused to pay the fine. She continued to campaign for women until the end of her life.

In 1870, the Fifteenth Amendment to the American Constitution gave black men the right to vote. Many people who had fought for the abolition of slavery went on to campaign for women's suffrage. Women were not given the vote in the United States until 1920.

◀ Cartoonists saw Susan and her fellow women temperance campaigners as waging a holy war against the demon drink.

Harriet Tubman
(1821-1913)

Harriet Tubman was born a slave in Maryland. From the age of 6 she had to work hard for her owner or be whipped. Harriet longed to escape to the north where she would be free, but she was 28 before her chance came. A Quaker woman who lived nearby heard that Harriet was about to be sold to the Deep South and told her of an escape route. Harriet took it.

For two nights and a day, Harriet walked, from Maryland into Delaware to the house she had been told of. Then, she walked again to Wilmington near the border with Philadelphia. Slave catchers were looking out for her, but, disguised as a workman, she walked straight past them to the home of another helper. The next night, she walked into Philadelphia.

Harriet often returned to the south to rescue groups of other slaves. She was still legally a slave herself, so she risked great danger. She rescued her brothers and even her parents. When slavery was at last abolished in 1865, Harriet continued to speak out for the rights of women and newly freed black people.

Harriet made nineteen journeys into the south, and led over 300 slaves to safety. When she was asked how it was she was never captured, she replied that she went only where God sent her.

◀ Harriet Tubman (far left, holding a pan) rests with some of the slaves whom she helped to escape. More of the escapers walked to freedom, although Harriet's parents, too old to walk, had to risk a train ride.

Catherine Spence
(1825-1910)

Catherine Spence was born in Scotland, but emigrated to Australia with her family when she was 15. Here, she became a successful novelist, a feminist and a reformer who helped children.

Soon after she arrived in Australia, Catherine got work as a governess and then started to write novels. In 1854, *Clara Morrison: a Tale of South Australia during the Gold Fever* was published, but not under her name. Two years later, her second novel appeared. She was the first successful woman novelist in Australia, and she continued to write for the next thirty years.

Catherine became concerned about children whose parents had died or could not look after them. They had to live, unloved, in large, strict orphanages. In 1872, she helped to form the Boarding-Out Society which tried to find families to care for the children instead. She herself looked after three families of orphans.

In the 1890s, she became more involved in politics. She campaigned for votes for women and for a better voting system. After women were allowed to vote in South Australia in 1894, Catherine continued to work for women's suffrage in other states and countries. In 1897, she stood for a seat in the Federal Convention, the first woman ever to do so, but she was unsuccessful.

As early as 1861, Catherine Spence argued that proportional representation (PR) was a fairer system of voting. Instead of parties simply winning or losing each seat, the seats are shared out between them according to the total number of votes they get. Many European countries now use PR, and many people in Britain want to introduce it.

▼ Catherine Spence cared for the poor women and children of Australia, and sought better rights for the Aboriginals (native Australians).

Olive Schreiner
(1855-1920)

Olive Schreiner was born on the southern tip of Africa. Her father was German and her mother English. Olive educated herself by reading books. She questioned her parents' religious beliefs and formed her own ideas, particularly about the position of women.

When she was 20, Olive started a novel, *The Story of an African Farm*. The story was published in 1884 under the pseudonym 'Ralph Iron'. Many people praised it, but many did not like it because it attacked Christianity and showed how women were oppressed.

In 1889, Olive returned to South Africa, which was ruled by the English. Olive thought this was unjust. When the English went to war against the Dutch Boers, who also lived in South Africa, Olive supported the Boers and was imprisoned. While in prison, she wrote *Women and Labour*, a book which still influences feminists.

The people who suffered most repression in South Africa were the black Africans, not the Boers. Later, the Boers themselves became the oppressors. It was not until 1994 that all South Africans, black and white, were allowed to vote to elect the first multi-racial government.

▼ During the Boer War in South Africa water was delivered to people in horse-drawn tanks.

Emmeline Pankhurst
(1857-1928)

Emmeline Pankhurst and her three daughters campaigned hard to persuade the government to give votes to women. Even as a child, Emmeline went to meetings with her mother where people argued for women's right to vote. In 1879, Emmeline married Richard Pankhurst, and they campaigned together until he died in 1898. Five years later, Emmeline and her daughter Christabel formed the Women's Social and Political Union.

They led marches and deputations to Parliament. Emmeline was a brilliant speaker, and many women joined them. In 1908, two suffragettes, as the women were called, threw stones through the windows of the Prime Minister's house in Downing Street. Emmeline was arrested for encouraging the suffragettes to break the law. During the next two

Many men were outraged at the idea of women being able to vote. They thought women were not clever enough to understand politics. As one man said, 'Votes for women, indeed: we shall be asked next to give votes to our horses and dogs!'

years, over 1,000 women were sent to prison. The campaigners became more angry and violent. Then in 1914, World War I began and Emmeline called a halt to the campaign. She encouraged the women to do men's jobs so that men could fight. Everyone could now see that women could work as well as men, and in 1918, Parliament agreed that women over 30 could vote. In 1928, the age was lowered to 21, making women equal to men.

◄ Emmeline Pankhurst is arrested during one of the suffragettes' protests in London.

Jane Addams
(1860-1935)

Jane Addams worked to make the world more peaceful, and the United States more fair and just to all its people. In 1931, she became the first woman to be awarded the Nobel Peace Prize.

In 1881, Jane started to train as a doctor, but had to stop because of an illness in her spine. Two years later, she toured Europe with her stepmother and returned for a second visit with a friend in 1887. She was appalled by the hopelessness of the slums she saw in the cities, but in London she felt she had found the answer in the settlement house, Toynbee Hall. She returned to the United States and bought Hull House in Chicago.

At Hull House, she offered people a place to live in a caring community. It was immediately successful. It quickly expanded to include local clubs offering nurseries, playgrounds and classes in English, fine arts and health. Jane was very aware of injustice and campaigned for trade unions, young people and for the rights of women. Settlements like Hull House were set up in other cities.

During World War I, Jane started the Women's Peace Party, and argued that the United States should not join the war. After the war, she continued to campaign for peace, immigrants, black people and others who were not being treated fairly.

Today, much of the work of settlement houses is done by social workers and social services. In Jane Addams' day, there were few welfare workers, day nurseries or playgrounds. Charities were the main source of help for needy people.

▶ Jane Addams travelled widely campaigning for peace. Here she leads an American group who were attending a Peace Congress at the Hague, in the Netherlands.

Maria Montessori
(1870-1952)

Maria Montessori had to fight to get an education, but she later devised a new way of teaching which helped children learn more easily.

Maria was born in Italy. Her father disapproved of her going to school, but luckily her mother helped her. In 1882, she went to Rome to study mathematics and engineering, but changed her mind, and in 1894, she became the first woman to graduate in medicine at Rome. She lectured in the psychiatric department of the university and became involved in teaching 'backward' children. These children were thought to be too stupid to learn, but Maria taught them to read and write by letting them learn for themselves without rules and discipline.

She entered several of the children for state exams and they did very well.

In 1907, Maria took charge of a nursery in a slum district of Rome and developed her new way of teaching so it could be used with normal children. She found that children learned better if they were free to explore for themselves, with the teacher's help. Unlike other schools at the time, Maria did not punish or reward the children. She wrote about her work and set up successful schools in Britain and the United States. After World War I Maria lectured about her methods and travelled, organizing colleges and training courses.

Maria Montessori's first Caso dei Bambini (children's house) was opened in Rome. There are now special Montessori schools in many countries of the world, but Maria's methods are also used in playgroups and nurseries everywhere.

◄ A Montessori teacher shows a child how to spell by using her sense of touch. The child is encouraged to feel the letters (which are cut out in rough sandpaper), so that she can learn to recognize their shape. Methods like this help children learn for themselves.

Maud Wood Park
(1871-1955)

Maud Wood Park was one of the leaders of the suffragette movement in the United States. As well as campaigning for the right of women to vote, she tried to improve the conditions of working women and children, and helped to organize the first Parent-Teacher Association.

Even before Maud had graduated from Radcliffe College in Massachusetts in 1898, Alice Birney had set up the National Congress of Mothers. Its aim was to get parents, teachers and the community to work together to put the needs of children first. In 1908, the organization was renamed the Parent-Teacher Association. Maud worked with the PTA, arranging for Boston schools to be used also as community centres.

The right to vote came gradually in the United States, state by state. Maud campaigned to get women the vote in the whole country. She lobbied Congress to amend the constitution, and finally in 1920, the Nineteenth Amendment was passed, giving all women the right to vote.

Maud Wood Park was married twice, but both times she kept her marriages secret. She married Charles Park in 1897 and Robert Hunter in 1908. This second marriage lasted until 1928. Why did she keep her husbands hidden? She must have felt she could campaign more effectively as a single woman.

▼ By the time this photograph was taken in 1922, Maud Wood Park (third from the right) was President of the National League of Women Voters.

Alexandra Kollontai
(1872-1952)

Alexandra Kollontai's father was a Russian aristocrat, but her mother's family were wood merchants in Finland. Alexandra turned away from the aristocracy and took up the cause of workers. She eventually became a member of the first communist government of Russia.

When Alexandra was 16 years old, she refused to become a conventional girl looking for a husband. Instead, she travelled around Europe. Four years later, she married her cousin, Vladimir Kollontai. In 1896, she went with him to inspect a large textile factory. She was appalled by the conditions the people had to work in. She was even more angry that Vladimir did not agree that the only way to make things different was to change the way the factory was owned and run.

Alexandra went to Germany to study economics. She thought it was wrong that a few rich men controlled the lives of so many people. In 1915, she joined the Bolsheviks, a group of people who wanted to overturn the rich ruling class in Russia and set up a state run by, and for, the workers. In 1917, the Russian Revolution did just that. Alexandra was made responsible for public welfare in the first Bolshevik government. But she soon fell out with the new leaders of Russia. They sent her abroad to work as a diplomat to keep her out of the way.

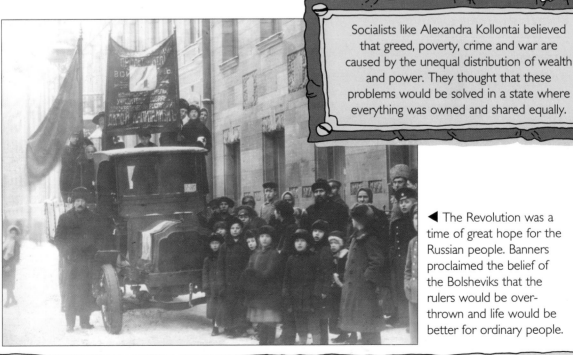

Socialists like Alexandra Kollontai believed that greed, poverty, crime and war are caused by the unequal distribution of wealth and power. They thought that these problems would be solved in a state where everything was owned and shared equally.

◀ The Revolution was a time of great hope for the Russian people. Banners proclaimed the belief of the Bolsheviks that the rulers would be overthrown and life would be better for ordinary people.

Marie Stopes
(1880-1958)

Marie Stopes thought it outrageous that she and most other women knew so little about sex and contraception. Her ideas caused an uproar in Britain but her books sold millions of copies.

Marie's mother was a feminist and one of the first women to have a university education. Marie too was very clever. At London University, she took three degrees at the same time, graduating in geology, geography and botany in 1903. She became an expert on fossil plants. She married a Canadian botanist, but their marriage was not a success. It took a year for Marie to realize that her husband was impotent, that is, he could not have sex with her. She was appalled that she knew so little about sex.

She read as much as she could about the subject, and in 1916, began to campaign for better sex education. In 1918, she married again and wrote her first book *Married Love*. Many women wrote to her, saying that they would enjoy sex more if they were not afraid of getting pregnant. This led to the book *Wise Parenthood*, in which Marie described different forms of contraception. In 1921 she and her husband opened a birth control clinic in London. In spite of opposition, she continued to argue for birth control.

Today, sex education is taught in school. When Marie Stopes was a child, however, adults did not tell children how babies were conceived and born. Instead of telling them the real 'facts of life', adults told children that a stork brought new babies or that babies were found under cabbage leaves.

▶ Marie Stopes continued her scientific work after leaving university, so that she could provide her campaign with facts and figures.

Jeanette Rankin
(1880-1973)

Jeanette Rankin was the first woman member of the House of Representatives in the USA. She spent the rest of her life campaigning for peace.

Jeanette grew up in Montana. She graduated in biology from Montana University in 1902, but then studied at the New York School of Philanthropy, and became a social worker in Seattle. Here, she could see very clearly the difficulties that women and families faced. She joined the suffragette movement to give women the right to vote and so have a say in the laws that governed them. When she was elected to represent Montana in Congress in 1917, she spoke up for laws to protect women and children, and she argued that the United States should not join World War I. In 1919, Jeanette lost her seat, but in 1941, she was re-elected and voted against the United States fighting in World War II. She continued to speak out against war for the rest of her life.

▲ A tireless peace campaigner, Jeanette Rankin spoke against the wars in Korea and Vietnam, as well as both World Wars.

Like Jeanette Rankin, many Americans opposed the Vietnam War. As the horror of the war was shown on television, more and more people joined the marches and demonstrations against the war, not only in the United States but in Britain and Europe, too.

▼ Many Americans joined Jeanette Rankin to campaign fiercely against the Vietnam War.

Margaret Sanger
(1883-1966)

Like Marie Stopes (see page 29), Margaret Sanger encouraged women to use contraception to limit the size of their families, and like her, she had to fight against fierce opposition.

Margaret's father was a stone mason. Her mother died at the age of 49, leaving eleven children. Such huge families were common in those days, since most women knew nothing about contraception. When Margaret grew up, she worked as a nurse in the slums of New York city. Here, she saw again how impossible it was for women with big families to escape from poverty and ill-health. In 1913, she went to Paris and met other people who believed that the best way out of poverty was to limit the number of children born. She returned to New York and distributed a pamphlet called *Family Limitation*, and in 1916, she opened a birth control clinic. It was soon closed down, and Margaret was imprisoned for 'causing a public nuisance'. Slowly the law began to change, however, and in 1921 Margaret formed the Birth Control League.

▲ Margaret Sanger was awarded the medal of the American Women's Association for her work. In spite of her influence, it was not until 1938 that US doctors were allowed to prescribe contraceptives.

Margaret Sanger organized the first World Population Conference in Geneva in 1927. At that time, there were about 2,000 million people in the world. Today, there are over 5,000 million. Many people fear that unless the increase is halted, famines and wars over scarce farmland will become more and more common.

◀ In 1917, Margaret Sanger's clinic in Brooklyn, New York, was closed down. She was charged and sent to the workhouse for thirty days. Here she waits with her supporters outside the court in Brooklyn.

Eleanor Roosevelt
(1884–1962)

Eleanor Roosevelt was more than just the wife of the President of the United States. She used her position to help people living in desperate situations. After World War II, she played a key role in getting forty-eight countries to agree to a Universal Declaration of Human Rights.

By the time Eleanor was 10 years old, both her parents had died. She felt unloved and very shy, until she went to school in England. Here she was valued because she was intelligent and kind, and she became more self-confident. She returned to the United States in 1902 and met her distant cousin, Franklin Roosevelt. They married three years later, and while Franklin started a career in politics, Eleanor settled down to be a mother. In 1921, however, Franklin became paralysed with polio, and Eleanor took over his political work until he recovered. In 1928, he was elected governor of New York, but the following year the Stock Market crashed, causing mass unemployment. In 1932, Roosevelt was elected president, promising to put people back to work. After his death in 1945, Eleanor continued on her own.

The Universal Declaration of Human Rights sets out the basic rights that all people have to be treated fairly and with dignity. It includes the right to freedom of thought, conscience and religion as well as the right to education, health care and employment. The Declaration does not make governments treat their citizens properly but it clearly shows when they fail to.

◀ After Franklin D. Roosevelt was elected President in 1932, Eleanor travelled the country, visiting sites like this camp for unemployed girls. She told her husband about the poverty and terrible conditions that she found.

Whina Cooper
(1895-1994)

As a Maori woman, Whina Cooper was not expected to speak in public, but she showed that she was as good as any man and she spoke up for Maori rights.

She was born in northern New Zealand in one of the country's poorest areas. Instead of playing games with the other children, she listened to the leaders of the tribes talking about who should own the land, the white people or the Maoris. Her father encouraged her, and the New Zealand government paid for her to go to college.

When Whina was 18 years old, a white farmer laid claim to the mudflats on which her Maori village was built. She organized a protest. She won, and for the next seventy years she took up the battle with other white land-owners. Some Maoris resented the fact that she was a woman, but Whina bred cattle and pigs, dug drains, and worked like a man. Younger Maoris wanted to take more violent action, but Whina believed that the two races should love each other.

▲ Whina Cooper wanted the white people of New Zealand to appreciate and understand the lifestyle, beliefs and culture of the Maoris.

Before European settlers landed in New Zealand all the land belonged to the Maoris. When Whina was 79, she and a group of 5,000 people walked 700 miles from her home in North Island to the capital city Wellington to protest against the fact that white settlers had taken all but four per cent of the land.

Helen Suzman
(born 1917)

In 1948, the Afrikaaner National Party were elected into power in South Africa. They believed that white people were superior to blacks and introduced the 'apartheid' system, segregating black and white people. Black people were forced to live on small areas of poor farm land, while white farmers kept the rest. Only Helen Suzman spoke out in parliament against these unjust laws.

Helen was born and brought up in South Africa. She graduated from university and became a lecturer in economics. At the same time, she worked as an unpaid social worker in the black townships. In 1953, she became an MP, and in 1959, she helped to form a new party, the Progressive Party. At the next election, however, she was the only member of the new party to be elected to parliament. Undaunted, she stood alone, day after day for many years, to criticize the government and to ask them awkward and embarrassing questions. In 1978, she was awarded the United Nations Human Rights Award.

Helen Suzman's Progressive Party believed that black people should be allowed to vote as well as white, but only if they had a certain level of education or wealth. The African National Congress, led by Nelson Mandela, insisted that all black adults should vote, and 1994 saw the first election in South Africa in which all black people could vote.

▼ Black people were forced to live in very poor conditions in the townships of South Africa. Helen Suzman was a lone white voice calling for greater racial equality.

Kath Walker
(1920-1993)

In 1964, Kath Walker became the first Australian Aboriginal to publish a book of poetry. She fought for Aboriginal civil rights and was awarded an MBE in 1970.

Kath Walker's mother was an Aboriginal and her father was German. She was born and grew up on North Stradbroke Island, just off the coast from Brisbane, and her childhood was steeped in Aboriginal tradition. Her mother could neither read nor write, but her father insisted that Kath was educated. Nevertheless, she left school at 13 and worked as a domestic servant in Brisbane. She wanted to be a nurse but was turned down because she was an Aboriginal. During World War II, she worked as an army telephone operator.

After the war, Kath married and had two children. She became more politically aware of the plight of Aboriginals. By 1961, she was State Secretary of the Federal Council for the Advancement of Aboriginals. She began to write poetry and her first volume *We Are Going* was soon followed by *The Dawn is at Hand*. Her poems emphasize the value of the Aboriginal way of life. She persuaded the government to change the constitution which discriminated against Aboriginals, and she continued to fight for their civil rights.

Many people were surprised when Kath Walker agreed to take part in the 1988 celebrations which marked 200 years of white settlement in Australia. She took the opportunity to take an Aboriginal name, Oodgeroo Noonuccal, and returned her MBE award, saying that Aboriginals had been in Australia for 10,000 years.

◄ When the Queensland state government wanted to reshape Moreton Bay on North Stradbroke Island, Kath Walker threatened them with the vegeance of Quandamooka, the water godess. She lived on the island for the last years of her life.

Maya Angelou
(born 1928)

Although she did not speak from the age of 8 to13, Maya Angelou became a singer, dancer, actress, teacher and writer. During the 1960s, she campaigned for the civil rights of black people.

Maya became used to struggle and hardship when she was a child. She was attacked by her mother's boyfriend and the shock left her mute for five years. When she was only 16, Maya gave birth to a son. The next year, she left school and took many different jobs to earn money to support her child. Soon she was making money as a singer and dancer. In the 1950s, she toured Europe and Africa with the musical *Porgy and Bess*. She has continued to work in films and theatre, not only as a performer but as a screenwriter, composer and director too. She lived in Ghana for several years, editing the *African Review*, and has observed the relationships between Afro-Americans and Africans, and between men and women. She comments upon the roles women play in American families and the importance of black women in their society.

Maya Angelou wrote several books about her own life. *I Know Why the Caged Bird Sings* describes her childhood. When she was three years old, Maya's parents divorced, and she and her brother were sent to their grandmother in Arkansas. They arrived by train with labels round their necks addressed 'to whom it may concern'.

▼ Maya Angelou's strength and energy have inspired many women, both black and white.

Cleopatra
(69-30 BC)

Cleopatra was a Greek, but she was the last pharaoh to rule over Egypt. She lived alongside the powerful Roman empire, and she knew that unless she got along with the Romans they were likely to conquer Egypt.

Cleopatra had to fight for her throne because her father had left it jointly to her and her brother. When Julius Caesar, the mighty Roman emperor, visited Egypt, he fell in love with Cleopatra and helped her defeat her brother and gain the throne for herself. Cleopatra gave birth to Caesar's son in 48 BC, and followed Caesar to Rome. Two years later, however, Caesar was assassinated and Cleopatra returned to Egypt.

After Caesar's death, Octavius and Mark Antony ruled the Roman Empire between them, Octavius in the west and Mark Antony in the east. Mark Antony invited Cleopatra to meet him, and he too fell in love with her beauty and wit. Instead of living with his own wife, he returned to Alexandria to live with Cleopatra in luxurious idleness. Many Romans distrusted Cleopatra. They thought she wanted to gain control over the eastern part of their empire, and they were right. Octavius and Cleopatra went to war, but Antony and Cleopatra were beaten in 31 BC at the Battle of Actium. Cleopatra was devastated. She knew that the Romans would now take over Egypt. To avoid being taken prisoner, she allowed an asp, a deadly poisonous snake, to bite her. When Antony heard of her death, he too committed suicide.

There are many legends about the life of Cleopatra. It is said that she first met Julius Caesar by smuggling herself into his camp, rolled up in a carpet or roll of bedding. She was hated by the Romans who insulted her and distrusted her as a scheming woman 'from the east'.

▶ Cleopatra lived in great luxury with Mark Antony in Alexandria, but together they planned to attack the Roman Empire.

Drusilla Livia
(58 BC–AD 29)

Drusilla Livia was the wife of Octavius, the first emperor of the Roman empire. When she was only 12 or 13 years old, Drusilla married her cousin Tiberius Claudius Nero. They had two sons, Tiberius and Nero. Drusilla was beautiful and very ambitious. When Octavius became emperor, he fell in love with Drusilla and ordered her to divorce her husband and marry him. She loved Octavius and, as she acted as his counsellor, she became powerful.

Octavius adopted his grandsons, Gaius and Lucius, as his own sons and began to favour their careers. Drusilla was not happy about this because she wanted her own son, Tiberius, to succeed Octavius.

When Agrippa, Gaius and Lucius' father, was murdered, it is thought that Drusilla may have been responsible. Tiberius was ordered to marry Agrippa's widow, although neither of them wanted to. However, when Gaius and Lucius died soon after, Tiberius became the natural successor. Tiberius became emperor in AD 14 but he resented his mother's continued interference.

Octavius and Drusilla had a large and splendid villa at Prima Porta, on the edge of Rome. You can still see the ruins of this villa today. The walls of one of the rooms are painted to look like an enchanted garden. They show orchards and flowerbeds with birds and insects among the leaves.

▼ This wall-painting comes from the finely decorated Villa of Livia on the edge of Rome.

Arwa bint Asma
(1052–1137)

Arwa bint Asma ruled the Yemen 900 years ago. Arwa's parents were king and queen in Yemen, but they died when Arwa was very young. She grew up at the court of her uncle and married her cousin, al-Mukarram, when she was 17 years old. In 1066, however, her uncle was assassinated while on his way to Mecca as a pilgrim. His wife was imprisoned, and it took nearly a year for her to get a message to her son. Al-Mukarram gathered an army to rescue her. He was so shocked to find out that his mother was safe and that he was now king, that he became partly paralysed and handed over power to Arwa.

One of the first things she did was to hunt down the man who had killed her uncle. Then she moved the capital from the coast into the mountains and gained power over the warring tribes. Once peace was restored, she encouraged farming and trade and made sure that all the taxes were collected. After al-Mukarram died in 1091, fighting broke out again, until Arwa agreed to marry Saba, the man who was to succeed her husband. But the couple never lived together.

Arwa bint Asma was one of several Muslim queens who ruled in the past. Although the Caliph of Baghdad stopped Shagrat al-Durr (see page 40) from ruling on her own, three sultanesses ruled in the Maldives. We know from the writings of traveller Ibn Battuta that Khadija, her sister Myriam and Myriam's daughter Fatima between them ruled there for forty years.

▼ The Queen Arwa Mosque, Yemen.

Shagrat al-Durr
(died 1258)

Shagrat al-Durr was a slave from the Turkoman area of central Asia. She became the favourite wife of the Caliph of Baghdad, Salih Ayyub, and ruled Egypt with him. After he died, Shagrat was determined to carry on ruling in Egypt, although to do so she remarried and then murdered her husband.

While Salih Ayyub was still alive, he spent much of his time fighting against the Christians in the Crusades. While he was away, Shagrat ruled in Egypt. The army liked her, and the generals were impressed with the decisions she made when her husband died. They agreed to keep his death secret, and she forged her husband's signature and collected an army to fight the French.

In 1250, Shagrat defeated the French king and imprisoned him. She then handed over power to her son, Turan Shah, but, unlike Shagrat and his father, he made a poor commander. He fell out with the army, and they assassinated him and made Shagrat queen instead.

She ruled by herself for only eighty days. Then, the Caliph of Baghdad decreed that a woman should not rule, and the army reluctantly agreed. They chose one of their generals, Izz al-Din Aybak, to rule instead. When Shagrat found out, she married him. They ruled together for seven years, until Izz al-Din decided to take a second wife, the daughter of a king. Maddened by jealousy, Shagrat had Izz al-Din murdered in 1257. Although some of the army remained loyal to her, she was beaten to death, and her body was flung over a cliff.

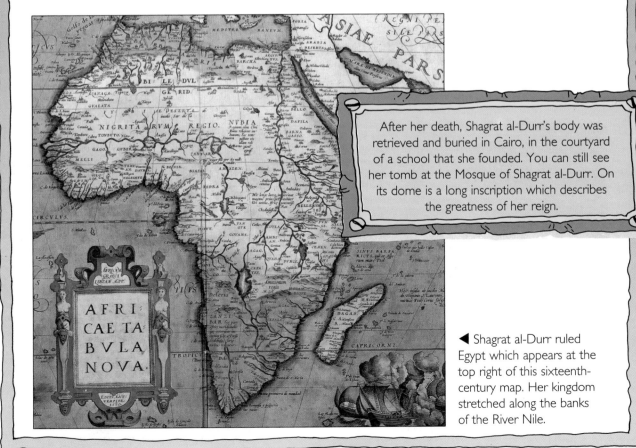

After her death, Shagrat al-Durr's body was retrieved and buried in Cairo, in the courtyard of a school that she founded. You can still see her tomb at the Mosque of Shagrat al-Durr. On its dome is a long inscription which describes the greatness of her reign.

◀ Shagrat al-Durr ruled Egypt which appears at the top right of this sixteenth-century map. Her kingdom stretched along the banks of the River Nile.

Jeanne d'Arc
(c. 1412-1431)

Jeanne d'Arc was just a girl of 17 when she led the French army to victory against the English. The English later captured her and burned her as a witch. To the French, she was always a heroine and a martyr, and in 1920, she was made a saint.

When Jeanne was a girl, England ruled much of northern France, and the French king and the Duke of Burgundy were at war. Voices told her that she must leave home and help the king of France regain his throne. The king had died and his son, the Dauphin, had not yet been crowned. Jeanne persuaded the local commander, Robert de Baudricourt, to take her to the Dauphin.

The Dauphin gave her a suit of armour and put her in charge of his army. The soldiers had heard about Jeanne and believed she had been sent from God to save them. Her army seized the town of Orleans from the English. Two months later, the Dauphin was crowned at Rheims. Jeanne continued to lead the French army against England and the Duke of Burgundy, but eventually they were beaten. Jeanne was captured and burned at the stake in 1431.

▲ The French were jubilant when Jeanne led their army to victory at Orleans.

In medieval times, when Jeanne lived, people still believed in witches. Many people feared Jeanne because she heard voices, and both Robert de Baudricourt and the Dauphin asked priests to question Jeanne to make sure she was not a 'devil's helper'.

Isabella I
(1451-1504)

When Isabella was born, Spain was divided into three main provinces, Aragon in the east, Granada in the south and Castile which occupied most of the rest. Isabella managed to unite these provinces into one country, Spain.

Isabella's father, Juan II of Castile, died when she was 3 years old and she was taken to the court of her step-brother Enrique. Enrique recognized Isabella as his heir, and was keen for her to marry someone who would strengthen his position, but Isabella made up her own mind. In 1469, she married Ferdinand, the heir to the throne of Aragon. One day, she planned, they would be joint rulers.

When Enrique died in 1474, Isabella had to act fast. He had in the end left his throne to his daughter, Juana. Isabella stepped in and quickly had herself crowned. Five years later, Ferdinand became king of Aragon. They each ruled their separate kingdoms but together they fought against the Muslims who

▲ Isabella and Ferdinand stand on either side of their daughter, who ruled over a united Spain.

Christopher Columbus asked Isabella to give him money to sail round the world. In 1492, she agreed, but, instead of reaching India as he intended, Columbus discovered the West Indies. His voyages led to the conquest of most of South America for Spain.

ruled Granada. Isabella herself took part in the campaign, until after ten years of fighting, they took Granada in 1492. When Isabella died, she left Castile to her daughter, Joan, knowing that she would be queen of the whole of Spain when Ferdinand died.

◀ The voyages of Christopher Columbus did not lead to India, but they did lead to great wealth for the Spanish monarchs.

Catherine de Medici
(1519-1589)

Catherine de Medici was born in Italy, but became the mother of three French kings, and through them had huge political influence in France.

Catherine's father was the wealthy and powerful ruler of Florence, but both her parents died soon after she was born. Catherine was brought up by two uncles who were both popes, and in 1533, when she was only 14 years old, she was married to the second son of the French king. After the death of his elder brother, Catherine's husband became Henri II, king of France, in 1547. Although Catherine was queen, her husband was in love with another woman so Catherine had little power over him. But when he died in 1559, Catherine came into her own. Her eldest son was king for only a year before he too died. Catherine became regent for her second, 10-year-old son, Charles. She tried to increase the power of the royalty by bringing peace to the warring groups of Catholics and Protestants. When Henry III, succeeded Charles in 1574, Catherine's influence declined. People were suspicious of her because she was Italian.

Although Catherine was a Catholic, she introduced a law in 1570 that allowed Protestants to practise their religion. This toleration did not last long, however, because two years later Catherine allowed Protestants to be killed in the Massacre of St Bartholomew. This attack was repeated all over France.

▼ Courtiers of Catherine's son Charles are entertained at the royal palace.

Elizabeth I
(1533-1603)

When Elizabeth was born, her father Henry VIII was furious that she was a girl. He wanted a son to become a king for England. However, when Elizabeth eventually became queen, she became one of the strongest and most successful monarchs in English history.

When Elizabeth was only 3 years old her mother, Anne Boleyn, was executed. After Henry's death, her step-brother, Edward, and then her older step-sister, Mary, took the throne. When Mary died in 1558, Elizabeth became queen and ruled for forty-five years.

Elizabeth was a clever ruler. She passed a law allowing Catholics and Protestants religious toleration, and she managed to stay at peace with France and Spain for thirty years. Elizabeth lived at a time when the closed world of Europe in the Middle Ages was opening up. Sailors were discovering new lands in the Americas and the East. Elizabeth encouraged Englishmen to trade with India and China.

Elizabeth never married. Her cousin, Mary, Queen of Scots, wanted to be queen of England too. Elizabeth imprisoned Mary, and eventually had her executed when it was proved she was plotting to overthrow Elizabeth. When Elizabeth died, however, it was Mary's son James who became king of Scotland and England.

In 1588, the peace with Spain broke down. The Spanish king sent a great fleet to invade England. Elizabeth herself gathered her army at Tilbury, near the mouth of the Thames and vowed to fight with them to save England. She didn't have to because her sailors, led by Francis Drake, defeated the Spanish fleet. Elizabeth was now queen of one of the most powerful nations at that time.

◀ Francis Drake was knighted by Queen Elizabeth I for bringing back gold from Peru and Chile. He also led two famous attacks on the Spanish Armada. In the first, he destroyed a large part of the fleet in Cadiz harbour. In 1588 he played a major role in the defeat of the Armada in the English Channel.

Maria Theresa
(1717-1780)

Maria Theresa's father was Charles VI, Holy Roman Emperor. He ruled a huge empire in central Europe which included Austria, Hungary and Bohemia. He had no sons and he wanted to leave all his lands to his daughter. To do so he had to pass a special law and persuade other countries in Europe to recognize her when she became ruler.

In 1736, Maria Theresa married Francis Stephen, Duke of Tuscany and they had sixteen children. When her father died in 1740 Maria Theresa took control of the empire. Despite their earlier promises, Prussia, Spain, Bavaria and France immediately claimed parts of her land.

Maria Theresa was an efficient ruler who introduced many reforms. She made it compulsory for children to go to primary school and she made prisons less harsh. When Francis died in 1765, Maria continued to rule with her son.

▼ Maria Theresa ruled with compassion.

The Holy Roman Empire was originally set up in 800 to defend Christian lands against the Muslims. Maria Theresa was a member of the Hapsburg family who ruled the Empire from 1440 until 1806, when Napoleon abolished it. Nevertheless the Hapsburgs continued to rule the powerful Austro-Hungarian empire until the end of World War I.

Catherine the Great
(1729-1796)

Catherine was a princess who was born in Prussia but became empress of Russia. She was an ambitious and energetic woman who made herself ruler of Russia in place of both her husband and her son.

Prussia wanted to make an alliance with Russia, so in 1744, the 15-year-old Catherine was married to Peter, the 16-year-old heir to Russia. Peter was weak and stupid and Catherine despised him. Like Catherine, Peter had been brought up in Germany and he hated everything Russian. Catherine saw how this annoyed the Russians and became as Russian as she could. She converted to the Russian Orthodox church in 1745, and gathered Russians around her at court. When Peter became Tsar in 1762, he changed the court to make it like Prussia. The Russian nobles were so angry they deposed him and made Catherine ruler. Peter was murdered a few days later, and, instead of becoming regent for her son, Catherine declared herself empress. The borders of Russia expanded as Catherine took over large areas of what was then Turkey and Poland.

Long after the rest of Europe had changed, Russia still had a feudal system. The serfs owed allegiance to the nobles and had to pay them large taxes. Their land was owned by the nobles and they had very few rights.

▼ Catherine is crowned in 1762. As a result of her conquests she was soon known as 'Catherine the Great'.

Victoria
(1819-1901)

Victoria was queen of Britain when it was the most powerful nation in the world. The British governed lands all around the world, giving it an empire 'upon which the sun never set'.

Victoria became queen when she was 18 years old. In 1840, she married her cousin, Albert, with whom she was very much in love, and with whom she had nine children. Victoria relied on Albert for help and advice. At that time, Britain was changing fast, and Albert was enthusiastic about all the new technology and trade. Cotton mills and steel mills were built, and towns quickly grew into cities. Britain was the first country to manufacture vast quantities of goods cheaply. Raw materials were brought in from the countries of the empire, and Britain became rich and powerful. With Albert's encouragement, a Great Exhibition was set up in Hyde Park, London, in 1851. A huge glass pavilion was built, called the Crystal Palace, and millions of people came to see the machines and new inventions. The most important visitor

Victoria insisted on good manners among her family and the people around her. One day, her son Bertie was late for dinner. He hid behind a pillar, sweating, before apologizing to her. She nodded curtly and he fled to hide behind another pillar for the rest of the meal. Extraordinarily, Bertie was 50 years old at the time!

was Victoria herself.

Ten years after the Great Exhibition, Albert died. Victoria was devastated and lived in seclusion for several years. Her popularity declined, but by the end of her life, she had regained it. When Victoria died, the whole empire mourned the passing of a great era.

◀ Queen Victoria arrives at the House of Lords to open the first parliament of her reign. The ranks of nobles and guardsmen admire the new young queen.

Ch'iu Chin
(c. 1879-1907)

When Ch'iu Chin was born, China had changed little since the sixteenth century. Women had no rights. If you were a woman, you had to obey your father until you married. Then, you obeyed your husband, and if he died, your sons.

Most women were not allowed to travel, but Ch'iu Chin's father was a government lawyer, and she travelled with him all over China. She saw how Chinese women lived and it made her angry. Unlike most Chinese women, Ch'iu Chin was well educated.

When Ch'iu Chin was 18, her father arranged for her to marry, and she moved to Peking. Like her, many people wanted China to change, but their efforts failed. In 1904, Ch'iu Chin left her husband and two children, and went to Japan for two years, where she joined a group of Chinese revolutionaries. She returned to China in 1906 and planned to overthrow the ruling Manchu family, but she was found out. In 1907, she was arrested and executed. Four years later, the Chinese Revolution, which Ch'iu Chin had dreamed of, succeeded.

▲ The empress was a member of the Manchu family that had ruled China for 300 years. Ch'iu Chin could question their traditional rule because she was educated. She had studied western history, and so knew that other lifestyles were possible.

The Chinese thought that women should have small feet, so little girls' feet were broken and then bound in tight cloth to stop them growing. This was a horribly painful custom which deformed their feet totally. Ch'iu Chin spoke out openly against foot-binding. She said it helped to make women into slaves.

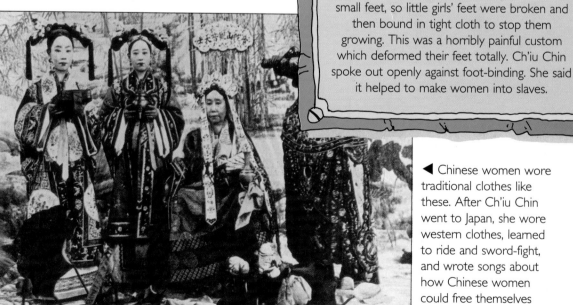

◀ Chinese women wore traditional clothes like these. After Ch'iu Chin went to Japan, she wore western clothes, learned to ride and sword-fight, and wrote songs about how Chinese women could free themselves from the rule of men.

Sirimavo Bandaranaike
(born 1916)

In 1961 the people of Sri Lanka elected Mrs Bandaranaike as the first woman prime minister in the world. In 1994, her daughter, Chandrika Kumaratunga became the fist woman to be elected president of Sri Lanka.

Sirimavo Bandaranaike did not study politics, but in 1956 her husband became prime minister. When he was assassinated three years later, to everyone's surprise, she took over as his successor and the following year she was elected as prime minister herself. Her socialist policies were not popular with everyone. In 1965 she lost the election, but was returned in 1970. Thousands of people rioted in the late 1970s, and a conservative leader took control, and made himself president.

Since 1983, the Tamils in the north of

▲ Mrs Bandaranaike's policies won her great popularity in rural Sri Lanka, although her government was defeated when there was a recession.

Unlike her mother, Chandrika Kumaratunga studied politics and development economics at a university in Paris. Like her father, her husband was assassinated; he was a leading figure in Sri Lankan politics and a famous film star.

Sri Lanka, have been fighting the government because they want to form an independent country. In the eleven years of conflict, more than 34,000 people were killed in bombing and fighting. In 1994, Mrs Bandaranaike's daughter, Chandrika, won the presidential elections, and promised to set up talks with the Tamil terrorists so that a peaceful solution could be found.

◀ Chandrika Kumaratunga, daughter of Mrs Bandaranaike, casts her vote in the 1994 election. She hopes to keep the support of those who backed her mother, while also starting talks with the Tamils.

Indira Gandhi
(1917-1984)

Indira Gandhi was India's first woman prime minister. Her father was Jawaharlal Nehru, the first elected prime minister of independent India.

Indira was always interested in politics. When she was 13, she organized a children's section of India's Congress Party and joined the party itself when she was 20. She studied at university in Bengal and Oxford. In 1942, she married Feroze Gandhi, a journalist.

When her father led India to independence in 1947, Indira became his political hostess and helper until he died in 1964. Indira was then elected to parliament herself. She toured India, speaking to enormous crowds and gaining their support. Two years later, she became leader of the Congress Party and prime minister.

Mrs Gandhi believed in democracy but ruled like a dictator. She wanted to fight poverty, but she became unpopular when she imprisoned political opponents and when her son, Sanjay, tried to force men to be sterilized as a solution to India's overpopulation problem. Mrs Gandhi called an election in 1977, but lost and was expelled from parliament. She again toured the country and regained her support. In 1980, she was re-elected prime minister. She had to deal with religious clashes and fierce opposition. She was assassinated in 1984, by her own Sikh bodyguard, after she ordered her troops to storm the Sikh temple in Amritsar.

Although the Indian people did not like Sanjay, Mrs Gandhi relied on his advice and help. After he was killed in an aircrash in 1980, Mrs Gandhi turned to her other son Rajiv. When she was assassinated, Rajiv was immediately sworn in as prime minister. He confirmed his position by winning the general election in 1984.

► Indira Gandhi inspects her troops. She relied on a strong military, but in the end she was killed by her own bodyguard.

Benazir Bhutto
(born 1953)

Benazir Bhutto was Pakistan's first elected woman prime minister. Her father was prime minister of Pakistan and leader of the Pakistan People's Party. Benazir survived a military coup to follow in his footsteps.

Benazir was born into a rich family. She studied at Harvard in the United States and at Oxford, where she excelled in politics. She seemed set for a dazzling career. In 1977, she returned to Pakistan and almost immediately found herself in the middle of a crisis.

Her father was deposed by the army and he, Benazir and her mother were imprisoned. In 1979, her father was executed on the orders of the military dictator General Zia. Benazir and her mother were held under house arrest which meant that they could not leave their home. In 1984, they were released on condition that they left the country. They went to London and together led the Pakistan People's Party (PPP). In 1986, Benazir returned to Pakistan and spoke out against Zia. Once again, she found herself in prison. In 1988, the General allowed democratic elections. Benazir led the PPP to victory, but her government was not a success. She lost the elections, in 1990 but was re-elected in 1993.

When Benazir Bhutto won the election in 1988, the opposing leaders claimed that it was 'unMuslim' for a woman to lead a country. They said that such a thing had not happened since Mohammed. They were wrong; as we know, Arwa bint Asma (see page 39) was one of fifteen Muslim queens to rule before Benazir.

◀ Benazir Bhutto rallies her supporters in Pakistan in 1988. Her party, the PPP, would soon take power.

Joice Nhongo
(born 1955)

When Joice Nhongo was born, her country was ruled by white people and was called Rhodesia. Joice joined a guerrilla army to fight for her country's independence, and in 1980, became a minister in the first black government of the new Zimbabwe.

Joice's family were very poor. Her parents were peasants, and Joice had eight brothers and sisters. She knew she could do little to help her family by staying at home, so she ran away to join the 'boys in the bush', a group of rebels who wanted to fight the white people who ruled the country and owned most of its wealth. Living in the wild was hard, but Joice put up with the discomforts and dangers, and showed that she was a good fighter. When she was only 18 years old, she became one of the leading members of the guerrilla army ZAWLA. Three years later, she was put in charge of the largest guerrilla-refugee camp in neighbouring Mozambique.

Joice married Rex Nhongo, the deputy head of ZAWLA, and she became ZAWLA's most famous and wanted guerrilla-fighter. The Rhodesian army were eager to capture or kill her. In 1978, their air force attacked the camp in Mozambique. Although Joice was pregnant, she fought back. Two days later, her daughter was born. Joice thought it was too dangerous to keep her baby at the camp so she sent her to live with friends in Zambia. She did not see her child again until 1980 when Rhodesia became the independent country of Zimbabwe.

▲ Many women guerrilla-fighters were inspired by Joice Nhongo, a leading member of Zimbabwe's guerrilla army. She later held various ministerial posts in the government.

The head of ZAWLA, Robert Mugabe, became the first prime minister of Zimbabwe, and Joice was appointed Minister of Youth, Sport and Recreation. She held the post only for a short time before becoming the Minister of Community Development and Women's Affairs in 1981.

▶ The first President of Zimbabwe, Robert Mugabe.

Mary bar Joachim
(c. 25 BC–c. AD 40)

Mary, the mother of Jesus Christ has been revered by Christians throughout the world for 2,000 years, yet little is known about her except what is written in the Bible.

It is thought that Mary was born in about 25 BC, and that her parents were called Joachim and Anna. The Bible says that she was a virgin when an angel appeared to her and told her that she was to give birth to the Son of God. When the baby was almost due to be born, Mary and her husband, Joseph, had to go from their village, Nazareth, to Bethlehem to be registered for tax. Bethlehem was crowded with other tax-payers, and Mary and Joseph could find nowhere to stay except a stable. Here, Mary gave birth.

Jesus grew up to preach a revolutionary message: that people should love God and each other. He was accused of being a trouble-maker and crucified by the authorities. Mary was one of the people who waited by the cross as Jesus died. She stayed in Jerusalem after the crucifixion, and may have died there a few years later.

Although so little is known about the real

▲ This sixteenth-century stained-glass window from an English church shows Mary holding the infant Jesus as the Magi, or three wise men, bring him gifts of gold, frankincense and myrrh.

Roman Catholics believe that Mary as well as Jesus was without sin. Nevertheless when he was 12 years old, Jesus gave Mary and Joseph a fright. Without telling them, he went to the temple in Jerusalem. His parents looked for him for three days before finding him there talking to the religious teachers. They were amazed by his understanding.

Mary, her character and the role she played in the life of Jesus have inspired artists and composers for hundreds of years. In the many famous pictures of her with Christ as a baby, Mary is shown as calm and loving. Catholics in particular regard her as a most special woman, second only to God and Jesus.

'A'ishah Bint Abi Bakr
(c. 613-678)

'A'ishah Bint Abi Bakr was only a child of 11 when she married the prophet Mohammed. After his death, and unusually for a woman, she became a powerful person in Muslim politics.

After Mohammed was driven out of Mecca, he travelled to Medina and set up the first community of Muslims there. The first thing he did was build a mosque and a house alongside it. Then he married 'A'ishah. She was the third and favourite of his nine wives, and he always defended her in any dispute. He died when she was 18 years old and she was not allowed to remarry.

'A'ishah was very intelligent and well educated. She became an expert on Muslim tradition. Mohammed had left no son to succeed him. 'A'ishah supported the claim of her father, Abu

▲ The city of Medina, where Mohammed went after he had been driven out of Mecca. In the middle of the city, with its large dome and courtyard, is the Mosque of the Prophet Mohammed.

The battle which 'A'ishah fought against the Caliph is known as the Battle of the Camel, because 'A'ishah, who was the only woman on the battlefield, rode a camel. After her defeat, the Caliph asked her why she had not stayed at home, where all women were expected to be.

Bakr, who was a fervent supporter of the Prophet, to become caliph, or leader. But Mohammed's son-in-law, 'Ali Ibn Abi Talib, became caliph. Many disagreed with his teachings, and 'A'ishah led a revolt. She spoke to the crowds, urging them to take up arms against the Caliph. In 656, she herself led thousands of men into battle against him. She lost the battle, and was captured. 'A'ishah's teachings led to the formation of the largest group of Muslims, the 'Sunnis'.

◀ The prophet Mohammed ascends to heaven. 'A'ishah was with the prophet when he died. Her intelligence, and her position as favourite wife of Mohammed, gave her great power after his death.

Mary Baker Eddy
(1821-1910)

Mary Baker Eddy founded a new Christian church, called Christian Science.

Mary grew up on a farm near Concord in New Hampshire, USA. She married in 1843 but her husband died less than a year later. She suffered from an illness of the spine and she was separated from her only child. As her troubles increased, she turned more and more to the Bible for help and comfort. In February 1866 she fell on the ice and injured herself badly. Her life seemed hopeless, but as she was reading in the gospel of Matthew how Jesus had healed a man suffering from palsy, she was suddenly healed herself.

She then searched the Bible for the laws of spiritual healing. In 1875 she published *Science and Health with Key to the Scriptures* and the following year she founded the Christian Science Association. Things moved quickly after that. In 1877

> Today there are 2,400 Christian Science churches in sixty-three countries. They teach that God is wholly good and that God's creation is the true reality. Whatever is unlike God - sin, evil, and sickness – is unreal. Christian Scientists believe that healing comes about through prayer.

she married Asa Eddy and two years later she set up The First Church of Christ, Scientist in Boston. It is called The Mother Church and she directed it until she died. Christian Scientists believed that Mary had been inspired by God. They study the Bible and Science and Health. Many local churches were built and more books published. The churches are run democratically. The services are conducted by members who have been elected to serve as readers. In 1908 Mary founded the newspaper *The Christian Science Monitor.*

◀ The First Church of Christ, Scientist is at the centre of a large group of buildings in Boston that house the church headquarters.

Marie Tussaud
(1761-1850)

Although wealthy women were not expected to earn money, the wives and daughters of tradespeople and merchants were expected to help with the business. Marie Tussaud not only helped to make wax models, she eventually ran the whole show and established Madame Tussaud's in London, an exhibition of waxworks which you can still see today.

Marie was born in Switzerland and lived with her widowed mother and her uncle, who was a wax-modeller. When Marie was 9 years old, they moved to Paris where her uncle set up a wax museum and a chamber of horrors. In the days before television and photographs, most people had no idea what the rich and famous (and infamous) looked like. They flocked to the waxworks exhibition to see. France was on the brink of revolution. Soon people were flocking to see the aristocrats being executed. Although Marie had spent many years teaching art to the royal family, she quickly changed sides and made masks of Marie Antoinette and other former friends after they were guillotined. She displayed them in the exhibition.

In 1794, Marie's uncle died, leaving her the business. The next year, she married Francis Tussaud but the marriage was unsuccessful. She kept his name, however, and brought the exhibition to Britain where she toured for over thirty years. In 1834, she set up a permanent exhibition in London, and, eight years later, passed the business over to her two sons.

Marie Tussaud made death masks by putting plaster over the face to make a mould. When the mould was dry and hard, she poured in the wax. You can still see some of her masks and models in Madame Tussaud's, including a model of herself.

▼ Historical scenes, often with an element of horror, were among the most popular of the subjects in Marie Tussaud's exhibitions. This one shows the execution of Mary Queen of Scots.

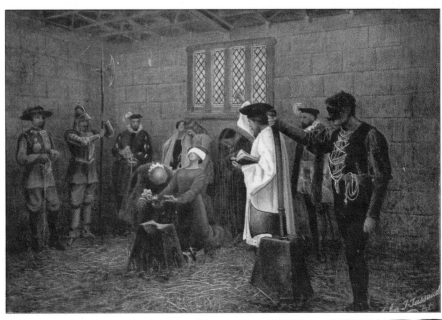

Coco Chanel
(1883-1971)

Coco Chanel could not sew, but she could pin and cut. Her clothes were revolutionary and made her one of the most successful fashion designers.

Coco Chanel's parents died when she was young, and she went with her sister to work in Deauville in northern France for a man who made and sold hats. In 1912, Chanel opened her own shop, but her hats were different. Instead of huge ones, decorated with fruit, feathers, bows and other trimmings, Chanel sold plain hats, and she wore one herself with simple, plain clothes. In 1914, she opened a shop in Rue du Cambon in Paris. At that time, most women wore long skirts and corsets which hampered their movements. Chanel liked clothes that were easy to wear and that she could 'jump into'. Her styles were just right for independent women looking for greater freedom after World War I. She brought in all sorts of innovations,

In 1931, Chanel was invited to Hollywood to design clothes for the American filmstar Gloria Swanson. They were not a great success, however, because as, the *New Yorker* magazine reported, 'She made a lady look like a lady. Hollywood wants a lady to look like two ladies.'

including cardigans, real pockets, artificial jewellery, Chanel No. 5 perfume and bell-bottomed trousers. She made a fortune.

Chanel remained in Paris during World War II, and some people thought she was too friendly with the Germans who occupied the city. They expected her to lose her popularity after the war, but she started a new fashion revolution. Previously, she had sold only to rich women. Now she made high-fashion available to everyone. She produced thousands of copies of cheap but well-designed clothes.

◀ Chanel's clothes were simple but superbly cut. Because they were 'easy to wear' they brought about a revolution in the way women dressed.

Mary Pickford
(1893-1979)

Mary Pickford was known as 'America's sweetheart', but this well-loved and famous filmstar was also a skilful business woman who formed and owned her own film company.

Mary Pickford was born Gladys Smith in Toronto, Canada. Her father was killed when she was just 5 years old. She worked as a child actress, and when she was only 14, she starred in a play on Broadway. Two years later, she started working for the film-maker D. W. Griffith. At that time, all the films were silent, but her expressive acting and good looks made her a star.

For the next six years, Mary moved from one film company to another and so increased her salary from $40 to $10,000. In 1916, she set up the Mary Pickford Corporation, and three years later she formed the United Artists Corporation with two other filmstars, Charlie Chaplin and Douglas Fairbanks, and with Griffith. Mary Pickford retired from the movies in 1933. In 1975, she was given a special Academy Award for her services to the film industry.

▲ Mary Pickford at the time of her wedding. When she and Douglas Fairbanks married, it seemed like a movie come true. But the marriage did not last.

Movies were big business in the 1920s and 30s. At first, only the pictures were shown, while a pianist played music. Mary Pickford made over 200 silent movies. It was not until 1927 that sound was introduced. Mary Pickford made four 'talkies', but they were not successful.

▼ Mary Pickford is surrounded by her staff. The company United Artists allowed Pickford, Fairbanks and Chaplin to control how their films were made.

Laura Ashley
(1925-1985)

Coco Chanel (see page 57) liberated women from Edwardian and Victorian fashions. Fifty years later, Laura Ashley made her name by re-introducing them.

Laura Ashley trained as a secretary when she left school, but in 1949, she married. When she became pregnant a few years later, she turned her kitchen into a printing workshop. She designed and printed cloth using a handmade silkscreen. She made the cloth into headscarves, and sold them to John Lewis, a big department store. The scarves sold so well that she started her own business with her husband.

Laura loved the styles and fabrics of the Victorian age. At first she produced smocks and aprons, but soon she was designing flowing skirts, high-necked blouses and dresses. She searched through museums to get ideas for her designs. Her business expanded all over the world. By 1985, Laura owned eleven factories and 225 shops, and her daughter and two sons were all involved in the business. She died suddenly after a fall when she was only 60 years old.

▲ Laura Ashley began her business in her kitchen. By the time of her death, she was producing furnishing fabrics and wallpapers as well as clothes.

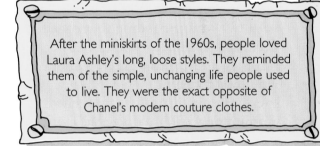

After the miniskirts of the 1960s, people loved Laura Ashley's long, loose styles. They reminded them of the simple, unchanging life people used to live. They were the exact opposite of Chanel's modern couture clothes.

▼ The designs of Laura Ashley's clothes are now known all over the world. This is just one of a chain of shops that covers Britain, Europe, and the USA.

Anita Roddick
(born 1943)

In 1976, Anita Roddick opened the first Body Shop in Brighton. She sold body creams and lotions made from natural products in small, refillable plastic containers. Ten years later, there were 1,000 Body Shops around the world. These shops demonstrated a new way of doing business.

Anita's parents were Italian, but she was born and grew up in Littlehampton in England. Before she opened the Body Shop, Anita and her husband Gordon ran a bed and breakfast hotel and a restaurant. Then, Gordon took two years off to ride a horse from Buenos Aires in Argentina to New York. Anita, with two young children to look after, decided that a shop would be easier to run than a restaurant. But her shop would be different.

As a student, Anita had travelled around the world, and she had noticed that ordinary women in New Guinea, Africa and elsewhere did not buy expensive cosmetics. They used local products such as cocoa fat and pineapple juice. She was irritated that the cosmetics industry spent so much money on packaging and advertising. She discussed her ideas with a herbalist and together they came up with a new kind of product. It was immediately successful.

> The Body Shop tries to do business in a way that is fair and honest, and helpful to the environment. It opposes testing cosmetics on animals, and, by using plants that grow in the rainforest, it encourages people not to cut down rainforest trees.

◀ Anita Roddick stands outside one of her chain of Body Shops. By trading fairly, using natural materials, and recycling her packaging, Anita Roddick has tried to make people aware of a new way of doing business.

Shikibu Murasaki
(c. 978–1031)

Shikibu Murasaki wrote *The Tale of Genji*. This long novel is not only the first of its kind to survive, but is still one of the world's greatest novels and probably the finest piece of writing in Japanese literature.

Shikibu was born into one of Japan's ruling families. Her father was governor of a province and must have been an enlightened man. He allowed Shikibu to study with her brother, something which was almost unheard of then. When she was about 20 years old, Shikibu married her cousin, a member of the Imperial Guard. They had a son and were very happy. But then things began to go wrong. Her husband died and her father was posted far away from the Kyoto Court where she lived. Shikibu did not want to leave her friends and life at Kyoto, but luckily her father managed to find a position for her with the Empress Akiko. Shikibu seems to have been a happy, intelligent person. She kept a diary between 1007 and 1010, and it is a lively account of people at the court. Her main work, the novel *The Tale of Genji*, was written to be read aloud. It tells the story of the loves and adventures of a prince and then of his son. There are fifty-four books and the work must have taken years to write. Shikibu was also well known as a poet.

In her diary Shikibu Murasaki commented on the other court ladies in a way that suggested she herself was a rather sharp-tongued person. She also spoke badly of her rival Sei Shonagon in her diary. Sei was author of the other brilliant classic of the time, *The Pillow Book of Sei Shonagon*, a book of impressions and reflections.

◄ Shikibu Murasaki was lucky. She had a talent for observation, a good education, and lived at the Imperial Court. These were excellent qualifications for writing a novel about the adventures of a prince.

Artemesia Gentileschi
(1593-c. 1642)

In most classical paintings, women are shown to be passive or coy. But Artemesia Gentileschi painted heroic women from history and from the Bible, such as Cleopatra and Judith, and showed them to be strong and powerful.

Artemesia was born in Rome. Her father was a painter, who recognized his daughter's ability and encouraged her painting. One of Artemesia's earliest works is *Susanna and the Elders*. In it, she shows Susanna surprised in her bath by two old men. The scene had been painted by other painters, but, instead of showing Susanna looking coy as they had, Artemesia chose to show Susanna distressed and vulnerable. Two years after *Susanna and the Elders* was painted, Artemesia's father accused her

Artemesia Gentileschi was one of several women painters who lived in Italy in the sixteenth and seventeenth centuries. Most of the others worked in Bologna where the university admitted women, and the patron saint, the abbess Caterina dei Vigri, was a woman painter.

teacher, Tassi, of raping her and of stealing some of their paintings. Although Tassi was acquitted in 1612, it is not clear whether he in fact seduced or raped Artemesia. The experience certainly seems to have made Artemesia more defiant and independent. In 1614, she moved to Florence where she married and continued to paint. Soon she was famous and was asked to paint pictures for the nobility.

◀ The Jewish heroine Judith, shown in this picture *Judith and Holofernes*, was one of Artemesia's favourite subjects.

Aphra Behn
(1640-1689)

Aphra Behn was the first woman to earn her living by writing. She led an adventurous life even before she started writing. Her husband died when she was still young and, apart from teaching and spinning, there were few ways she could earn money respectably. In 1666 she went to Antwerp as a spy for King Charles II. He ignored her information and did not pay her, so she was sent to prison for debt. Here she began to write.

Her first play, *The Forced Marriage*, was a lively comedy about sex and politics. It was performed in 1670, and was followed by several other plays, novels and poems. Her most successful play, *The Rover*, was first performed in 1677. In 1688, she wrote *Oroonoko*, about slavery in Surinam . She was the first person to attack slavery in this way, and the first to write about a black hero.

Aphra Behn's work was very popular at the time, although she herself was often criticized and insulted for daring to write, something which only men

Aphra Behn's work was largely ignored until recently. She and Eliza Haywood were both among the first people to write novels, but Daniel Defoe and Samuel Richardson are usually said to be the first novelists.

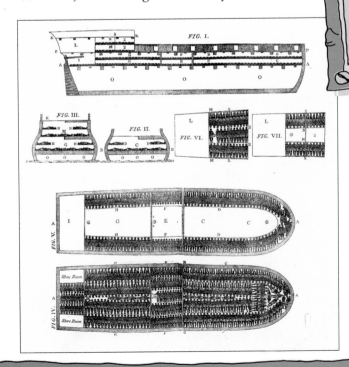

were expected to do. She wrote openly about sex, and by Victorian times, her work was thought to be too shocking to be read.

◀ There was no room to move on board a slave ship, as these storage plans show. Aphra Behn was ahead of her time in attacking the inhumanity of slavery.

Jane Austen
(1775-1817)

Jane Austen is one of the greatest English novelists, but few people knew of her during her lifetime. Her books were published anonymously, and she hardly made any money from them.

Jane's father was a vicar, and Jane was the sixth of seven children. She went to school for less than three years, but was taught at home by her father. She started to write short stories and plays when she was only 10 years old. We know a great deal about the way Jane and people like her lived, because she describes them so precisely in her novels.

In 1801, her father retired and the family moved to Bath, which Jane hated. By this time, Jane has already had her first novel, *Elinor and Marianne*, published. She later rewrote it as *Sense and Sensibility*. Her father tried to get the novel which was later called *Pride and Prejudice* published but was not successful. In 1803, another novel, *Northanger Abbey*, was bought by a publisher for a very small fee, but he did not actually publish it.

Women were not expected to earn money in Jane Austen's day. They had to depend on their husbands for money, and economic security was more important than love. Many of Jane Austen's books describe the way in which mothers tried to arrange 'suitable' husbands for their daughters.

◄ A scene from a film production of *Pride and Prejudice*. Jane Austen's books have a very wide appeal, and many of them have been made into films.

George Eliot
(1819-1880)

Mary Anne Evans wrote some of the best novels in the English language, but few people know her name. That is because she published them under a man's name: George Eliot.

Mary Anne was born in Warwickshire and went to school in Coventry, where she learned German, Italian, Latin and Greek. When her mother died in 1836, she took over the running of the house. She was very religious, but in Coventry she met free-thinkers and began to doubt her beliefs. She translated philosophy into English, and moved to London in 1851 to work on a magazine called the *Westminster Review*.

In London, she fell in love with George Henry Lewes, a writer and critic. They could not marry, however, because Lewes' wife would not divorce him, so they lived together instead. This was considered shocking and unacceptable then, and for several years, Mary Anne was an outcast from society. Lewes encouraged her to write fiction and in 1856 she started *Amos Barton*. By 1858, she had ready a collection of short stories, *Scenes from Clerical Life*. Although women were accepted as writers of romances and popular fiction, they were still not accepted as serious writers, so she took the name George Eliot. She went on to write *Daniel Deronda, Middlemarch*, and many other highly praised novels. She became the most famous woman writer of her time.

Many women writers took men's names. The Brontë sisters first published under the names Currer, Ellis and Acton Bell. Literary critics knew that women did this and would try to guess whether an author was male or female. If they thought that a book was written by a female author, the critics always judged it more harshly.

Clara Schumann
(1819-1896)

Clara Schumann was a famous pianist and a composer. She married the composer Robert Schumann, and played and publicized her husband's work more than her own.

Clara's father was a pianist, composer and piano teacher. He taught her to play the piano when she was very young, and when she was 11, he took her on her first concert tour. That first tour was followed by others, and by the time she was only 16, Clara was famous throughout Europe. Her playing was admired by royalty and by composers such as Chopin and Mendelssohn.

Meanwhile, Clara had fallen in love with Robert Schumann, one of her father's pupils. In 1832, he had broken a finger and could no longer play, but he continued to compose music instead. Clara's father did not want them to marry and kept taking Clara away on long European concert tours, but Clara and Robert married in 1840. Although she eventually had eight children to look after, Clara carried on playing, teaching

and occasionally composing. Her main works were her Piano Concerto written in 1836 and her Piano Trio composed in 1847. She had little confidence in her compositions, however, and helped to promote the work of Chopin, Brahms and her husband instead.

It was not unusual for children of 9 or 10 to give concert performances as Clara did. Mendelssohn gave his first public performance when he was 10, Chopin when he was 8 and Mozart when he was only 6 years old.

◀ Clara Schumann was well known as a pianist in her youth, but devoted much of her life to others. When she was older she turned more and more to teaching. She was appointed to the post of principal piano teacher at the Frankfurt Conservatory in 1878. She also edited her husband's music for publication.

Jenny Lind
(1820-1887)

Jenny Lind was one of the world's most popular opera singers. People used to stand outside her house in London and beg her to sing. She was known as the 'Swedish Nightingale'.

Jenny was born in Sweden and began singing at the age of 10. She sang first in vaudeville, but then trained at the Royal Opera School in Sweden. She sang her first operatic part when she was 18, but her voice had become overstrained. She had to rest before going to Paris for further lessons. In 1842, she returned to Sweden and began a highly successful career in Germany as well as in Sweden.

In 1847, she came to Britain to sing the role of Alice in *Robert le Diable*. It was the event of the year. Queen Victoria, Prince Albert and Felix Mendelssohn went to the first night, and at the end of the performance, Queen Victoria threw her own bouquet of flowers on to the stage at Jenny's feet.

Jenny Lind toured in the United States but eventually settled in Britain. Her voice was pure and controlled and audiences adored her. She seemed to light up when she sang. Three times, the House of Commons was brought to a standstill because so many of its members had gone to the opera to hear her. In 1883, she retired from the stage, and became professor of singing at the Royal College of Music.

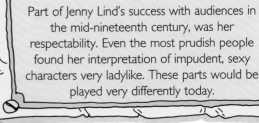

Part of Jenny Lind's success with audiences in the mid-nineteenth century, was her respectability. Even the most prudish people found her interpretation of impudent, sexy characters very ladylike. These parts would be played very differently today.

◀ Jenny Lind was always in demand during her singing career. This nineteenth-century cartoon shows her 'exchanging her notes for gold'. After her retirement, as well as teaching, she often took part in concerts to raise money for charity.

Emily Dickinson
(1830-1886)

Emily Dickinson was a great poet who lived her life as a recluse, talking to no one but her family and close friends.

She was born in Amherst in Massachusetts where her father was a lawyer. He dominated Emily and her sister Lavinia and ruled every part of their lives. Even when they were adults, he would not let them buy their own books or chose their own friends. After Emily left school, she never left Amherst. She always dressed in white and stayed at home. She started writing poetry when she was about 30 years old. She wrote on odd scraps of paper which she sewed together into small books. In 1862, she sent some poems to the critic and writer Thomas Wentworth Higginson, but he did not understand her style, although he rather pompously encouraged her. After that, Emily would not show her work to anyone.

In 1884, Emily developed kidney trouble and became an invalid. Before she died, she told her sister to destroy all her poems. Lavinia found more than 1,700 poems hidden away in trunks and drawers but could not bring herself to burn them. Instead, she sent them again to Higginson who edited them with Mabel Loomis Todd, a friend of Emily's. They were published in three volumes but they were not generally liked. It was some time before she was recognized as a poet of great intensity and originality.

Emily Dickinson's poems are so full of awe, longing and despair that people have wondered whether she might have had a secret but hopeless passion for a man or woman. Some have even wondered whether it might have been Higginson himself, but there is no evidence to prove it.

Sarah Bernhardt
(1844-1923)

Sarah Bernhardt was one of the most famous actresses of all time. She was so beautiful and graceful, and acted with such expression that she was known as 'the divine Sarah'. She played male parts as well as female and continued to act until she was nearly 80 years old. Sarah was born in Paris in France, and went to acting school when she was 13 years old. She was not an immediate success. In 1862, she got a small part at the Comédie Française, but no one took much interest in her. She then tried her hand as a singer, but still without success. However her luck changed in 1869, when she played the part of a wandering minstrel in François Coppée's *Le Passant*. During the next three years, she made her name playing important roles in plays by Shakespeare and Victor Hugo. People praised her for her 'golden voice' and for the emotional power of her acting. She toured the United States and performed in England and Denmark. Sarah's love-life was as dramatic as her performances. She was married once but only for a short time. In 1898, she bought her own theatre in Paris and named it the 'Théâtre Sarah Bernhardt'. Although she was now over 50 years old, she played the part of Hamlet and went on to be a huge success in *L'Aiglon*.

In 1905, Sarah Bernhardt injured her leg while performing in Rio de Janeiro. The injury became worse, and in 1915, the leg was amputated. Undaunted, Sarah continued to act with an artificial leg, but sat down throughout her performance.

◀ Sarah Bernhardt was perhaps the most versatile actress of all time. As well as the heroines of the great French classical tragedies, she is one of the few women to have played Shakespeare's *Hamlet*.

Ethel Smyth
(1858-1944)

When she was 18 years old, Ethel Smyth astonished her parents by wanting to study music. Ethel's father, an officer in the British army, did not approve of his daughter's ambition to become a professional musician. Ethel, however, locked herself in her bedroom and refused to talk to anyone until they agreed to let her study at the Leipzig Conservatory in Germany. There, she studied composing as well as the piano.

In 1893, her *Mass in D* was performed at the Royal Albert Hall in London. The critics were amazed that this important work had been composed by a woman. Ethel went on to write many other works including several operas. In 1903, *The Wood* was the first opera written by a woman ever to be performed at the Metropolitan Opera House in New York. Her most famous opera *The Wreckers* was first performed in 1910. Apart from her work as a composer, Ethel also made a terrific contribution to the suffragette movement. In 1922, she was made a Dame of the British Empire.

Ethel Smyth was a fervent suffragette. She wrote an anthem called *The March of the Women* and was sent to prison for throwing stones at a cabinet minister's window. While in prison, her fellow prisoners sang the anthem while Ethel conducted with a toothbrush!

▼ Ethel Smyth conducts the Metropolitan Police Band at the unveiling ceremony for a memorial to the suffragette Emmeline Pankhurst in London.

Anna Pavlova
(1885-1931)

Anna Pavlova came from a poor family in Russia, but she became one of the world's most famous ballet dancers.

Anna's father died when she was only 2 years old, and Anna herself was not a healthy child. Nevertheless, after seeing a performance of *The Sleeping Beauty*, she was determined to become a dancer. When she was 10 years old, she was thrilled to be accepted by the Imperial Ballet School. In 1903, she danced in *Giselle*, and three years later became a leading ballerina with the Russian ballet company, Ballets Russes. Anna worked immensely hard. Her technique was superb and her performances were magnetic. The dance *The Dying Swan* was created especially for her. She toured through Europe and was adored

Anna Pavlova and the Ballets Russes took Europe by storm. Everyone felt that Russians made the best dancers. British dancer Hilda Boot changed her name to Butsova. Alice Marks changed hers to Alicia Markova.

wherever she went. In Denmark, a group of admirers pulled her carriage through the streets.

In 1912, Anna bought a house in London, and the following year, she started her own ballet company. The company was managed by Victor Dandré, and together they travelled 300,000 miles and gave nearly 3,000 performances. In 1930, Anna Pavlova danced in Britain for the last time. The next year, she caught a chill and died of pneumonia.

◀ Anna Pavlova was famous for her superb technique and her appealing presence on stage. Her success took her all over the world from Hollywood to India.

Virginia Woolf
(1882-1941)

Virginia Woolf was at the centre of a group of writers and artists called the Bloomsbury group. They defied the social rules of the time, and Virginia defied literary rules to write in a new kind of way.

She was born in London into a wealthy family, but before she was 20 years old, her mother, stepsister, elder brother and father had all died. She moved into a house in Bloomsbury with her sister Vanessa and her two brothers. At that time, Bloomsbury was a run-down area, but the house became a meeting place for writers, painters and other friends.

In 1912, Virginia married Leonard Woolf, and they began their own publishing business, the Hogarth Press.

She also started to write. Her first novel, *The Voyage Out*, was published in 1915, and she continued to write novels and stories for the rest of her life. In 1929, she wrote *A Room of One's Own*, a non-fiction book in which she explored the reasons why so few women were able to write and why their work was less well known than men's. She concluded that women need their own space and money to be free to be themselves.

Virginia's mental health was always fragile. She suffered from depression and had several nervous breakdowns. In 1941, she drowned herself.

In her novels *The Waves* and *To the Lighthouse*, Virginia Woolf wrote using a technique known as 'stream of consciousness'. Instead of telling a story with a strong plot, she explored the minds of her characters.

◀ *Orlando*, also written by Virginia Woolf, was made into a film in the 1990s.

Marian Anderson
(1902-1993)

Marian Anderson started singing for the local Union Baptist Church when she was only 6 years old. Nearly fifty years later, she became the first black person to sing at the Metropolitan Opera House in New York.

Marian Anderson was born in Philadelphia. Her family were poor but their religious faith was strong. The followers of the local Union Baptist Church loved her singing and realized that her voice was special. They raised the money for her to have singing lessons. When she graduated from high school, Marian moved to New York to study further. In 1925, she decided to enter a singing competition. Her rich voice rose and fell. The audience applauded loudly, but 300 other people were also competing. Marian waited and waited. At last, the winner was announced: Marian Anderson!

Her powerful voice could reach very high and very low notes. It was just right for operatic parts, but people were not used to black people singing in operas. Marian toured Europe and became famous in London, Sweden and Germany before she was invited to sing in the United States. She made her debut in New York in 1936, but her difficulties were not over. In 1939, she was barred from singing at Constitution Hall in Washington because she was black. Eleanor Roosevelt (see page 32) arranged a separate concert for her at the Lincoln Memorial instead. Marian carried on singing until she was 63 years old, and received many awards.

In 1956 Marian Anderson's extraordinary life story was published – it is called *My Lord, What a Morning*. In 1958 President Eisenhower made her a delegate to the United Nations.

▶ Marian Anderson was one of the first black singers to become involved in opera. Her talent was widely recognized and helped to break down racial barriers.

Barbara Hepworth
(1903-1975)

Barbara Hepworth broke away from the traditional ways of sculpting to become one of the most famous sculptors of the twentieth century.

Even as a child, Barbara wanted to be a sculptor. She grew up in Wakefield, Yorkshire, and studied at the Leeds College of Art, the Royal College of Art in London and in Italy. She was closely associated with other sculptors including Henry Moore and her first husband, John Skeaping.

In the 1930s, she, along with Henry Moore and her second husband Ben Nicholson, became interested in the modern art of Picasso, Mondrian and others. Barbara was one of the first to create abstract sculptures. In 1939, she moved to St Ives, Cornwall where her work was influenced by the landscape, the sea and the sky as well as stone circles and other ancient monuments. She used string in her wood sculptures to create harmony and tension. After the

▲ *Three Personages*, a slate sculpture of 1965, which now stands in Kettle's Yard, Cambridge.

war, her work became famous worldwide, and she was asked to create a large sculpture for the UN Building in New York. Barbara continued to work into old age. She died in a fire in her studio in St Ives. This is now a small museum devoted to her work.

Carving a sculpture from marble is hard work. Controlling the hammer and chisel takes great skill. Although her arms often ached, and her fingers were bruised and bleeding, Barbara Hepworth loved the sound of the hammer. She said she could tell how well a piece was going by the 'music' of the hammer.

◀ Dame Barbara Hepworth in her garden in St Ives, Cornwall.

Simone Weil
(1909-1943)

Simone Weil was born in Paris. Her parents were intellectual, Jewish and middle-class. When she graduated in 1931, instead of continuing an academic career, she decided to live like a poor and uneducated person. She worked as a farm labourer and in a car factory. Like the communists, she believed that workers were exploited, but, unlike other left-wing intellectuals at the time, she realized that communism would not solve the problems of working people. She hated the tyranny of both the left and the right.

When the Spanish Civil War broke out, Simone went to Spain to fight for the Republicans against the fascists. In World War II, when Paris was occupied by the Nazis, she moved to London to join the Free French fighters. From the late 1930s, she began to have mystical experiences and became interested in Catholicism. She was known as the 'Catholic saint outside the Church'. She decided to eat the same diet as the prisoners working in Nazi labour camps. She was not strong enough, however, and soon caught tuberculosis and died.

▲ Simone Weil was born in Paris. She was a philosopher who believed in religion and socialism. She cared passionately for the poor and oppressed.

Simone Weil's writings were published after she died. Many of her ideas have yet to be taken up. In her essay *Factory Journal*, she argues that workers need to control their own factories and that machinery and working systems should be redesigned to make them more humane, that is, less painful to work with.

Simone de Beauvoir
(1908-1986)

Simone de Beauvoir was born in Paris and studied philosophy at the Sorbonne University in Paris. Here, she met Jean-Paul Sartre. They became lovers but did not marry, because they wanted their relationship to be free and did not agree with the idea of marriage. Simone taught in Rouen, and Sartre at Le Havre. During World War II, Simone lived in Paris, and her first novel *She Came to Stay* was published in 1943. She wrote philosophical essays and two more novels. Her best known, *The Blood of Others*, was published in 1945.

Four years later, *The Second Sex* was published. This book explores the relationship between men and women, and points out that it is men who set the standards and that women always feel 'second best'. Simone wrote that marriage and motherhood were traps used by men to oppress women. There was an uproar. At that time, governments wanted women to give up their wartime jobs and become housewives again, leaving the jobs for soldiers returning from the war. Simone's book inspired many women who wanted to be treated equally to men.

During the 1950s and 60s, Simone became sympathetic to communism and supported the Algerians in their war of independence against France. In the 1970s, as feminism grew in strength, she campaigned for abortion and spoke on behalf of battered wives, single mothers and working women.

▲ Simone de Beauvoir upheld feminism through her writing, by founding a feminist journal, and as President of the League for the Rights of Women.

Simone de Beauvoir and Jean-Paul Sartre were existentialists. They believed there is no God. Instead people have to create their own truth, and, by their actions, they create their own being.

Nadine Gordimer
(born 1923)

Nadine Gordimer was born in South Africa and went to university in Johannesburg. She saw the unjust way that black people were treated by white people. Most white people ignored these injustices, but Nadine wrote about them in short stories and novels which showed how peoples' lives are poisoned by such racial prejudice.

Nadine's father was a Jewish refugee from Latvia who ran a store in a rough gold-mining town in the Transvaal. In 1948, the Afrikaaner National Party came to power, and racial persecution increased. The following year, Nadine published her first collection of short stories, and four years later, her first novel, *The Lying Days*. It is based on her own life, and describes the experiences of the heroine as she struggles to free herself from the racial prejudices of the mining town where she lives. Nadine Gordimer could have left South Africa and lived abroad, but she chose to stay and continue writing, although one of her books was banned by the Nationalist government.

Nadine Gordimer missed school for several years. Her mother imagined that she had a heart murmur and kept her at home. It was only later that Nadine found out there was nothing wrong with her heart.

▼ Nadine Gordimer attends a commemoration of black victims of police violence in South Africa.

Maria Callas
(1923-1977)

Maria Callas was one of the world's greatest opera singers. Her own life was often as colourful and dramatic as that of the characters she played on stage. Her full name was Cecilia Sophia Anna Maria Kalogeropoulos. She was born in New York but, by the time she was 15, her Greek parents had separated and Maria returned to Greece with her mother. She studied singing in Athens and gave her first performance in 1941.

During World War I she stayed in Athens, singing at the Athens Opera. After the war, she returned to the USA hoping to continue her career, but she was disappointed. In 1947, she was asked to sing in Ponchielli's *La Gioconda* in Verona, Italy. She was a great success, and during the 1950s, she sang in all the major opera houses around the world. But she always sang on her terms. If she thought her performance was not good enough, she would break her contract and not appear upsetting many theatre managers.

Her private life was also turbulent. In

Maria Callas was a legend in her own lifetime. She not only sang superbly, she was a vivid actress. She brought out the emotion and meaning in every part she sang. Her last stage performance was as *Tosca* in Covent Garden in London.

1949, she married her manager, but they broke up ten years later when she became involved with Aristotle Onassis, the Greek shipowner. That relationship ended unhappily when Onassis married Jackie Kennedy, the widow of the American President Kennedy. In 1965, Maria gave her last stage performance, but eight years later, she sang again in a series of recitals. She spent the last years of her life alone in Paris.

◀ Maria Callas in the title role of Puccini's *Tosca*, at the Royal Opera House, Covent Garden, London.

Janet Frame
(born 1924)

Janet Frame is New Zealand's greatest novelist. Her books reflect her own painful life. She was born in Oamaru, and had three sisters and a brother who suffered from epilepsy. The family was poor, especially during the years of the Depression, but Janet did well at school and became fascinated with literature. While she was still at school, she was devastated when her elder sister died in a drowning accident. A few years later, another sister drowned too.

Janet was extremely shy at college and university, and the strain of learning to teach led to a breakdown. She was sent to a mental hospital where she was told, wrongly, that she was suffering from schizophrenia, a serious and incurable mental illness. She spent seven years in a mental hospital being given regular electric shock treatment. Had she not published a book of short stories which won a major award, she would probably have spent the rest of her life there.

After her release, Janet wrote and published her first novel, *Owls Do Cry*. She lived in London and Spain for seven years, and wrote five more books. While in London, she asked to be admitted to a mental hospital, where she was told that she had never been schizophrenic. She returned to New Zealand in 1963, and has continued to write.

Janet Frame's first novel *Owls Do Cry* is about a family of four children who search through the town rubbish dump to find treasure. Much of it is based on her own life, as became clear when she wrote her own autobiographies in the 1980s. They were made into the film *An Angel at My Table* in 1990.

▼ A scene from the film *An Angel at My Table*, a very influential film, not only written by a woman, but also directed by a woman.

Margaret Atwood
(born 1939)

Margaret Atwood is Canada's most important and popular writer alive today. She has written many books of poetry, short stories and novels, and is well known internationally as a feminist writer.

Margaret was born in Ottawa but she spent most of her summers until she was 12 among the unspoilt forests and lakes of northern Ontario and Quebec. Her father studied insects and ran forest stations there. In 1946, Margaret's family moved to Toronto where she went to high school and university. She started writing as a child, and her first collection of poetry, called *Double Persephone* won a prize in 1961, but her work was not really recognized until *The Circle Game*, a collection of poetry, was published in 1966. She writes simply and directly, but her poems are strange and haunting.

She has lived and worked in many countries apart from Canada, doing a variety of jobs from waitressing to lecturing in universities. She is best known for her novels, which explore the emotions and dilemmas of liberated women and their relationships with men. Her first novel, *The Edible Woman*, is a satirical comedy about a woman who realizes that her personality is being eaten away by her relationship with her fiancé. She has won many prizes and awards for her work.

In 1972, Margaret Atwood wrote a book called *Survival: A Thematic Guide to Canadian Literature*. In it, she surveyed and criticized Canadian writers. Many people disagreed with her opinions, and many thought that she had included too many women.

Mary Somerville
(1780–1872)

Mary Somerville's family, like many others, thought girls should not be educated. Mary ignored what people thought and taught herself. When she was 15, she became intrigued by an algebra problem in a magazine. She began to listen to her brother's maths lessons as she sewed in the same room, and studied books.

Her first husband disapproved of clever women, but died three years after their marriage, leaving Mary enough money to be independent. She continued to study mathematics and astronomy. In 1812, she married William Somerville, an army surgeon. He encouraged her work and introduced her to other scientists in London. In 1826, she presented a paper to the Royal Society which described her experiments in solar magnetism.

She was regarded as an academic freak by both men and women, but Mary's abilities were at least recognized. She was asked to translate many foreign books into English and wrote her own books and papers. The Royal Society placed a bust of Mary in its hall.

When Mary Somerville died in 1872, women were still not allowed to study at universities in Britain. But seven years later, several women succeeded in establishing a college just for women at Oxford. They named it Somerville College.

◀ Somerville College, Oxford was founded in 1879. It was one of the first places in Britain to provide university-level education for women.

Ada Augusta
(1815-1852)

Ada Augusta, or Ada Countess of Lovelace, as she was also known, was the daughter of the English poet Lord Byron, but she was brought up by her mother, a strong-willed mathematician who was determined to educate her daughter. She employed a Cambridge academic to teach her but Ada also taught herself from books. She wanted to be a famous scientist.

In 1834, she heard about the work of Charles Babbage who had designed a mechanical calculating machine. Ada was intrigued. To find out more, her husband had to join the Royal Society, because women were not admitted, so that he could copy out information from books and papers for her. Ada became a friend of Babbage. She translated his work and added her own descriptions of how the

All her life, Ada struggled with migraines and ill-health. Although today's school exams show that girls often get the best results, most people in Ada's day thought that women's minds were too weak to learn. Even Ada herself thought that her illness was caused by 'too much mathematics'.

computer might work. She also devised several mathematical programmes of her own. But a great deal of money was needed to build Babbage's machine. Ada devised what she thought was a foolproof system for backing horses, but it did not work. She secretly pawned the family jewels to pay her debts and was blackmailed. Over a hundred years later, however, her mathematical achievements were remembered when the high-level computer programming language ADA was named after her.

◀ The large calculating machines that Babbage and Ada developed were full of brass cogs and levers, and were very expensive to make. They never finished their project, but some of their ideas are used by computer programmers today.

Maria Mitchell
(1818-1889)

Maria Mitchell grew up in Nantucket in New England where she was educated by her father. She helped him with work on navigational instruments on whaling ships and, when she was 13 years old, she helped him find the longitude of the town by making exact timings during an eclipse of the Sun. She became Librarian of Nantucket Atheneum when she was only 18 years old and continued with her study of astronomy.

Maria rocketed to fame in 1847 when, with the help of only a small two-inch telescope, she discovered a new comet. The comet was named *Miss Mitchell's Comet*, and she was awarded a gold medal by the King of Denmark. Her success brought recognition and more success. The following year, she became the first woman to be elected to the American Academy of Arts and Sciences, and she was employed by the US Nautical Almanac Office to compute changes in the planet Venus. She also helped other women. When the Vassar Female College was founded, Maria became professor of astronomy there. She helped to found the American Association for the Advancement of Women and became its president.

Comet Mitchell was a rare visitor to the night sky. Its glowing tail of melted gas could be seen only between 2 October 1947 and 8 January 1948 before its orbit around the Sun took it back into outer space.

◀ It was almost unthinkable in the nineteenth century for a woman to carry out the sort of scientific work that made Maria Mitchell famous. Maria was an obvious choice for the professorship of astronomy at the new Vassar Female College.

Elizabeth Blackwell
(1821-1910)

Elizabeth Blackwell was born in England, but moved to the United States when she was eleven years old. She wanted to be a doctor, but could not train because women were not allowed into universities or medical schools. Elizabeth decided to apply anyway. She was turned down by one medical school after another, until Geneva College in New York asked the medical students to vote on whether she should be accepted. The students thought it was a joke and agreed. When Elizabeth graduated in 1849, 20,000 people came to watch her receive her degree, but to gain hospital experience she had to go to London and Paris where she studied midwifery.

She returned to the United States in 1851, but still no hospital would employ her. Instead, she opened a clinic in one of New York's slums. She was joined by two other women doctors, her sister Emily and Marie Zakrzewska. They opened a small hospital for women and children. But Elizabeth really wanted to establish a medical college just for women. In 1868, the Woman's Medical College of New York Infirmary opened with Elizabeth as Professor of Hygiene. In 1869, she returned to England and helped to set up the London School of Medicine for Women.

Elizabeth Blackwell was not the first woman doctor. A doctor James Barry graduated from Edinburgh School of Medicine in 1812, and went on to practise as an army surgeon at the Battle of Waterloo and in South Africa. No one realized that Dr Barry was a woman until her death in 1865.

Elizabeth Garrett Anderson
(1836-1917)

Like Elizabeth Blackwell, Elizabeth Garrett Anderson wanted to be a doctor, but only men were allowed to train at the British medical schools. She took up nursing so that she could learn from operations and dissections. In 1860, she was allowed unofficially to train at the Middlesex Hospital, and she did so well that the male students asked for her to be removed. On finishing the course she qualified as an apothecary, the only medical qualification open to women.

In 1866, she opened a dispensary for women in London. Four years later, she graduated in medicine in Paris, but still the British Medical Association (BMA) would not recognize her. She began to work as a surgeon and with the help of her husband she turned the dispensary into a hospital for women. In 1873, the BMA finally recognized her.

▲ When she was accepted by the British Medical Association, Elizabeth went on to become president of the London School of Medicine for Women.

Even though women were sometimes admitted to lectures they were often banned from laboratories and dissecting rooms. When studying in London, Elizabeth Garrett Anderson had to dissect corpses on her own because she was not allowed into the dissecting rooms.

▼ When the University of Paris opened its doors to women in 1868, Elizabeth learned French and qualified as a doctor there.

Sonya Kovalevsky
(1850-1891)

Sonya Kovalevskywas born in Moscow into an aristocratic family. From the age of 14, her main interest was mathematics. She studied at St Petersburg and belonged to a group which argued for the emancipation of women. She married when she was 18 so that she could go with her husband to Germany to study physics. When her husband returned to Russia, Sonya went on to Berlin to study mathematics under Karl Weierstrass. The university would not admit women so Weierstrass tutored Sonya in private.

Although she wrote three papers on mathematics and was awarded a doctorate from Göttingen University, Sonya still could not get an academic job. She returned to Russia to live with her husband, but he committed suicide in 1883. Then Sonya's career made a breakthrough. The University of Stockholm appointed her lecturer in mathematics, and she wrote a paper called *On the Rotation of a Solid Body about a Fixed Point* which won a prize from the French Academy. The next year, she was made professor at Stockholm and was elected a member of the Russian Academy of Sciences.

▲ In 1888 the French Academy awarded Sonya their famous prize, the Prix Bordin. They were so impressed with her work that they raised the value of her prize from 3,000 francs to 5,000 francs.

When she was a child, Sonya's family friends included the famous Russian novelist Dostoevsky. After her daughter was born in 1878, Sonya wrote a book about her own childhood called *The Sisters Rajevsky*.

Marie Curie
(1867-1934)

Marie Curie was one of the world's greatest scientists and the first person to receive two Nobel prizes. Although she never realized it, her work killed her.

Marie was born in Poland and educated by her parents. Women were not allowed to study at university there, so Marie worked hard to send first her sister and then herself to Paris to study. She graduated in physics and in mathematics, and in 1895, married another scientist, Pierre Curie.

Henri Becquerel had discovered the mysterious energy, or radiation, given off by uranium. Marie decided to research this. She discovered that pitchblende was more radioactive than uranium, and found it contained two previously unknown elements. The first she called polonium, after Poland, and the second radium. No one believed radium existed, so for years, Marie and Pierre boiled tonnes of pitchblende to extract a tenth of a gram of pure, glowing radium. In 1903, it was discovered that radium could cure cancer, and Marie, Pierre and Becquerel were awarded the Nobel Prize for Physics. Pierre died in 1906, but Marie continued with her work and gained a second Nobel Prize.

Marie and Pierre both suffered from radiation sickness without knowing what it was, and Marie eventually died of leukaemia. Her notebooks are still so radioactive you would have to wear special protective clothing to read them.

▼ Marie Curie explains her discovery of radium and polonium. She was the first woman professor of the Sorbonne University, Paris.

Lise Meitner
(1878-1968)

Lise Meitner was a talented scientist but, as a Jew and a woman, she had to overcome two sources of prejudice. She succeeded, becoming professor of physics at Berlin and doing vital work which led to the splitting of the atom.

She first studied radioactivity in Vienna, where she was born, but moved to Berlin in 1907. However, one of the professors there would not allow her into the laboratories. Instead, she and Otto Hahn, a chemist, built their own laboratory in a carpenter's workshop and used it to measure radiation.

Hahn and Lise worked together for thirty years. When World War I broke out in 1914, Lise joined the Austrian army as a nurse and radiographer, and Hahn was called up to the German Army. During their leaves, however, they managed to continue their work and discovered a new chemical element, protactinium. After the war, Lise returned to Berlin, and she and Hahn went on working together, bombarding uranium with neutrons, until Lise was forced to flee from the Nazis in 1938. She went first to the Netherlands and then to Sweden where she and her nephew, Otto Frisch, wrote a paper suggesting that the bombardment of uranium had split the nucleus of the atom, a process called nuclear fission.

When other scientists learned about nuclear fission, they formed a team to develop a nuclear bomb. They invited Lise Meitner to join them but she refused and hoped that the project would fail. However, on 5 August 1945, the first atomic bomb was dropped on Hiroshima, Japan.

▶ The first atom bomb explodes in southern New Mexico, USA. Lise Meitner was against this use of nuclear fission.

Amalie Noether
(1882-1935)

Amalie Noether was a brilliant mathematician who wanted to lecture at university. She could only do so, however, as a last-minute replacement for a male lecturer.

Amalie's father was professor of mathematics at the university in Erlangen in Germany. Amalie, who was known as Emmy, was also interested in mathematics. In 1907, with the help of a family friend and tutor, Paul Gordon, she wrote a research thesis in algebra. Professor Noether's students were sometimes surprised to find that instead of the great man himself, his lectures were given by his daughter. They were even more surprised to find that her lectures were mathematically more interesting and exciting than his.

When her father retired, Emmy could no longer teach at Erlangen. Instead David Hilbert persuaded her to come to

Göttingen where she continued her research in mathematics, particularly the mathematical equations that make up Einstein's theory of relativity. This university would not employ her as a lecturer either, but with Hilbert's help she got round this. A lecture was announced under Hilbert's name, but given by Emmy! It was not until 1922 that the university finally accepted her, but on a very low salary. She published a paper with another mathematician and gradually her contribution to abstract algebra was recognized.

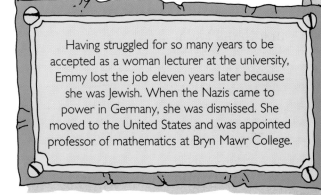

Having struggled for so many years to be accepted as a woman lecturer at the university, Emmy lost the job eleven years later because she was Jewish. When the Nazis came to power in Germany, she was dismissed. She moved to the United States and was appointed professor of mathematics at Bryn Mawr College.

◀ A Nazi rally. When the Nazis came to power in Germany in the 1930s, many Jewish people lost their jobs and, like Emmy, fled to the United States.

Irène Joliot-Curie
(1897-1956)

Irène Joliot-Curie, the elder daughter of Marie Curie (see page 87), followed in her mother's footsteps, in studying radiation and winning a Nobel Prize, and in other ways as well.

It is not surprising that Irène was interested in physics and radiation since she was taught science by Marie and her friends from the Sorbonne University in Paris. During World War I, Irène and her mother set up a mobile X-ray truck to treat wounded soldiers, and after the war Irène worked at the Radium Institute in Paris. She studied alpha rays from polonium for her doctoral thesis.

Irène was a shy woman, but she fell in love with Frédéric Joliot, a cheerful and exuberant physicist who also worked at the Radium Institute. Like Pierre and Marie, Irène and Frédéric not only married but formed a working partnership. By bombarding aluminium with alpha-particles, they created the first artificial radioactive element. This pioneering work was later used both in medicine and industry. In 1935, Irène and Frédéric were awarded the Nobel Prize for Chemistry. But Irène, like her mother, did not realize that she should protect herself from the lethal rays she worked so close to. She died of leukaemia in 1956.

▲ Irène Joliot-Curie did important work on radioactivity. She also argued for the right of women to become members of the French Academy of Sciences.

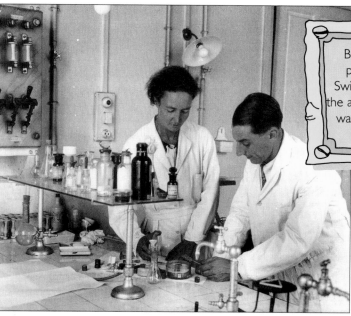

Both Irène and Frédéric were anti-Nazi and pacifists. During World War II, they fled to Switzerland. Having seen nuclear fission used in the atom bomb, they returned to France after the war and helped to establish the use of nuclear fission as a peaceful source of energy.

◀ Irène and Frédéric Joliot-Curie at work in their laboratory at the Radium Institute in Paris. Both owed their interest in radioactivity to working with Irène's mother, Marie Curie.

Charlotte Auerbach

(1899-1994)

Charlotte Auerbach was Jewish and German. Her work in Britain during World War II made her world famous amoung geneticists.

Charlotte was a school teacher but when the Nazis came to power in 1933 she was dismissed from her job and fled to Britain. Soon after she arrived in there, Charlotte obtained a job at the Institute of Animal Genetics in Edinburgh. When World War II broke out in 1939, the government thought that the Germans might use chemical weapons against them. Charlotte, working with another scientist, studied how mustard gas produced deadly changes in the genes. Charlotte's work was so secret, she could not use the name mustard gas, but had to call it 'substance H'. After the war, Charlotte's research was published, and she received many honours.

She continued to study gene mutation in great depth and considered this to be her most valuable work.

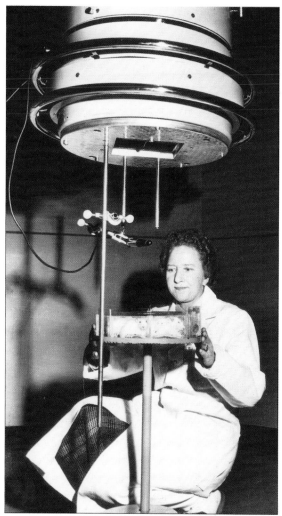

▲ Charlotte with a device designed to expose mice to doses of radiation. She proved that radiation could cause cancers such as leukaemia.

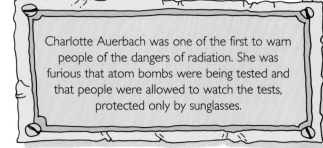

Charlotte Auerbach was one of the first to warn people of the dangers of radiation. She was furious that atom bombs were being tested and that people were allowed to watch the tests, protected only by sunglasses.

◄ Charlotte studied gene mutation in fruit flies at Edinburgh. Fruit flies breed very quickly and the changes (mutations) brought about by alterations in their genes are easy to see.

Margaret Mead
(1901-1978)

Margaret Mead was an anthropologist. She lived among people of other cultures and studied how they lived. Margaret graduated in anthropology in 1923 and went to study the people of the South Pacific. She spent nine months in Samoa, talking to and researching teenage girls. Then she wrote *Coming of Age in Samoa*. It caused a stir because it seemed to question the strict way in which children were brought up in the West.

Margaret's next trip was to New Guinea where she studied children under 5 years of age. Her book *Growing up in New Guinea* was another bestseller. It showed that if adults pay no attention to children, they grow up with little imagination or creativity. Altogether she wrote over forty books and over 1,000 articles.

▼ Margaret Mead with some of her subjects. She studied how children are brought up and how work is divided between men and women.

In 1933, Margaret Mead studied the Tchambuli people in New Guinea. She found that there the usual male and female roles were reversed. Men painted and danced, while women organized and ran society. It wasn't until thirty years later, however, that male and female roles in the West began to be challenged.

Barbara McClintock
(born 1902)

Barbara McClintock is a geneticist who received a Nobel Prize for her work on 'jumping genes'. But in the beginning, she had to struggle against her family to become a scientist at all.

Barbara was born in Connecticut in the United States, where her father was a doctor. When she was 6 years old, the family moved to Brooklyn, and Barbara became interested in science at school. Her parents disapproved, however, thinking it unsuitable for a girl, and her mother would not let her go to college. Barbara got a job and studied at nights and weekends instead. In 1919, she was accepted at Cornell University to study biology. It was here that she developed an interest in genetics.

With two other geneticists, Barbara researched chromosomes in maize and gained a PhD in 1927. As a woman, she found it difficult to get a good university job, but from the 1940s she worked at the Cold Spring Harbor Laboratory near New York. It was during this time that she realized that some genes control other genes, and that some, which she called 'jumping genes', can change position over several generations. In 1951, this conclusion was so unexpected that other scientists called her crazy, but in the 1970s work in molecular biology showed that she was correct. Only then was her work recognized.

Barbara McClintock was 81 years old before she received a Nobel Prize for work she had done thirty years earlier. She was the first woman to receive an unshared prize in medicine or physiology.

◄ This African violet contains a 'jumping gene', a type of gene that can change position. This plant would normally have had only pink flowers, but as a result of the gene that has changed position, one of the blooms is purple.

Kathleen Lonsdale
(1903-1971)

Kathleen Lonsdale was a Quaker and a scientist who believed passionately that science should be used to help people, not harm them. She encouraged women to become scientists, and she is most famous for her own work with molecular crystals.

She was born Kathleen Yardley in Ireland, the youngest of ten children. She was brilliant, even as a child. She won a scholarship to a girls' school but had to go to a boys' school for lessons in science and maths. When she was only 16 years old, she was accepted at London University, and she obtained the highest marks in ten years when she graduated in 1922. One of the examiners asked her to join his research team. Kathleen studied the structure of atoms and molecules by passing X-rays through different crystals and examining the different patterns they made. In 1929 she discovered that the carbon atoms in benzene are arranged in a hexagon. She also used X-rays to measure how far apart the atoms in a diamond are. Lonsdaleite, the diamonds found in meteorites, are named after her. Kathleen received many honours and became the first woman to be elected as a Fellow of the Royal Society.

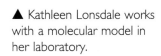

▲ Kathleen Lonsdale works with a molecular model in her laboratory.

▼ This computer drawing shows part of a crystal of lonsdaleite. The substance is not as hard as diamond.

Kathleen Lonsdale spent a month in prison during World War II. As a pacifist, she refused to register for Civil Defence, and was fined £2. When she refused to pay the fine, she was sent to prison.

Maria Goeppert-Mayer
(1906-1972)

In 1963, Maria Goeppert-Mayer received the Nobel Prize for Physics. She was the first woman to be awarded the prize since Marie Curie (see page 87) won it in 1903.

Like Marie Curie, Maria Goeppert was born in Poland. Unlike Curie, however, Maria was able to study in her own country and received a doctorate from the University of Göttingen in 1930. The same year, she married Joseph Mayer, an American physical chemist who was visiting Poland, and in 1931 she emigrated to the United States.

Maria worked with uranium, studying how its isotopes separated, but in 1945 she moved to Chicago and became interested in nuclear physics. Each atom consists of a nucleus of nucleons orbited by electrons, rather like a sun and planets. Some nuclei have a 'magic number' of nucleons, and Maria wondered why these nuclei were more stable than others. She developed the idea that the nucleons in the nucleus are arranged in shells. Magic-number nuclei have full shells of nucleons, making them more stable.

As often happens in science, another scientist, working quite independently, came up with the same idea. Hans Jenson and Maria shared the Nobel Prize.

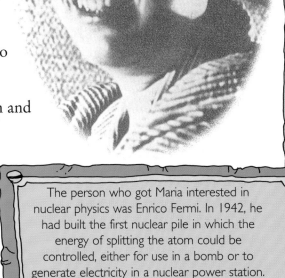

The person who got Maria interested in nuclear physics was Enrico Fermi. In 1942, he had built the first nuclear pile in which the energy of splitting the atom could be controlled, either for use in a bomb or to generate electricity in a nuclear power station.

◄ The structure of an atom. Electrons (shown in blue) orbit a tiny central nucleus. The nucleus is made of particles called protons (shown in red), and neutrons (green), held together by nuclear force.

Rachel Carson
(1907-1964)

Imagine spring with no birds. No noisy dawn chorus, no fish in the streams and no calves, piglets or chicks on the farms. In her book, *Silent Spring*, Rachel Carson said that each of these things had already happened somewhere in the United States. She predicted that they would happen everywhere if people did not stop poisoning the land.

Rachel was born in Springdale, Pennsylvania. Even as a child, she was fascinated by nature, and she wanted to be a writer. In college, she specialized first in English composition, but then changed to biology and genetics.

In 1936, she joined the US Fish and Wildlife Service as a biologist and editor. She studied marine life, and became very concerned about what she found. In 1941, she wrote *Under the Sea-Wind* and, ten years later, *The Sea Around Us*. She showed how the sea was being poisoned by industrial chemicals.

▲ When Rachel Carson's book *Silent Spring* was published in 1962, it became a bestseller, not only in the United States, but in other countries too.

◀ Rachel collected information from scientists all over the world about how the deadly poisons which farmers used to kill pests and weeds were upsetting the balance of nature.

Some of the most poisonous chemicals which Rachel Carson studied, such as DDT, have now been banned in Europe and North America. They are still used in poorer countries however. In *Silent Spring*, Rachel argued that safe, biological methods should be developed to control pests.

Dorothy Hodgkin
(born 1910)

Even before she was 10 years old, Dorothy Hodgkin was interested in chemistry. In 1964, that interest, a lot of hard work and intellectual understanding won her a Nobel Prize.

Dorothy was born in Cairo, but went to school in England and then to Oxford University. Here she became fascinated with the structure of molecules. A molecule is made up of atoms. Each atom is joined to one or more of the others, so that together they build into a complex structure, so small that even the most powerful microscope then available could not detect it.

Like Kathleen Lonsdale (see page 94), Dorothy used X-rays. She shone them through the crystal and photographed the pattern they made. Dorothy worked out the structure of penicillin using this method, and three years later, she began to analyse vitamin B12. It has over ninety atoms, and it took her eight years. The insulin molecule has over 800 atoms. In 1972, with the help of modern computers, she was able to reconstruct its incredible structure.

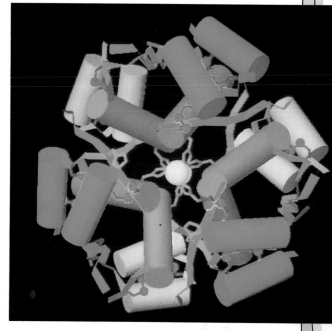

▲ Dorothy Hodgkin worked out the structure of penicillin and vitamin B12 using X-rays.

Dorothy Hodgkin received many honours. She was elected to the Royal Society in 1947, and became the first woman since Florence Nightingale to receive the Order of Merit. She used the money from her Nobel Prize for a scholarship, for peace and for the relief of famine.

◄ Dorothy Hodgkin was recognized for the contribution she made to the world of molecular chemistry. In 1964 she was awarded the Nobel Prize for Chemistry.

Mary Leakey
(born 1913)

Mary Leakey is an archaeologist who has spent much of her life sifting through dust and stones in Tanzania looking for the ancestors of today's human beings. Mary was used to travelling. Her father was a painter and Mary did not receive a regular education. She was good at painting herself and interested in archaeology and the earliest human beings. She attended lectures at London University, and when Louis Leakey asked her to join his archaeological expedition to Africa in 1935, she jumped at the chance.

Mary and Louis were married the following year and spent most of their lives looking for early hominids in East Africa. In 1959, while working in the Olduvai Gorge, Mary found a skull which dated from nearly two million

▲ Mary Leakey with some of the fossilized remains of early hominids that she has uncovered. Her work changed our ideas about human origins.

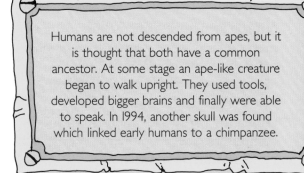

Humans are not descended from apes, but it is thought that both have a common ancestor. At some stage an ape-like creature began to walk upright. They used tools, developed bigger brains and finally were able to speak. In 1994, another skull was found which linked early humans to a chimpanzee.

years ago and was thought to be a missing link between modern humans, known as *Homo sapiens*, and earlier forms of upright hominids.

Mary carried on working in Tanzania. In 1976, she found two sets of hominid footprints, fossilized in volcanic ash. They proved that our pre-human ancestors walked on two legs nearly four million years ago, much longer ago than people had previously thought.

◀ Mary Leakey works on her excavation at Laetoli, Tanzania, where the famous trail of hominid footprints was found in 1976.

Jocelyn Bell
(born 1943)

Jocelyn Bell (Burnell) was working as a research student for the astronomer Antony Hewish in Cambridge when she noticed something new in deep space: regular bursts of radio waves. For three years, Hewish had investigated the sources of radio waves in space. The waves fluctuated like the twinkling light of stars. In 1967, Jocelyn began to study each source. Two months after she started, she noticed something strange, a source which emitted large, regular fluctuations. This new kind of star was called a pulsating radio star, or pulsar.

People wondered how such regular signals were made. Were they sent by some other form of life on a distant planet? Astronomers scoured the skies, and found other pulsars, so far apart that they couldn't have been made by aliens.

▲ An artist's impression of a pulsar. The astronomer Thomas Gold came up with an explanation of these mysterious objects. A pulsar is a spinning neutron star which emits radio waves rather like a lighthouse emits flashes of light. Antony Hewish shared a Nobel Prize for his work on pulsars, but Jocelyn Bell was not recognized for her contribution.

> Pulsars are very small, but give off huge amounts of energy. They may be no more than thirty kilometres across. Gold's suggestion that they are spinning neutron stars would mean that they consist only of the heavy centre of atoms, closely packed together.

Elizabeth Macarthur
(1766-1850)

Elizabeth Macarthur sailed to Australia in 1789 aboard a convict ship, but she was not a convict. She was born into a Devonshire farming family and received a good education. The voyage to Australia was not easy. She wrote to her parents telling them about the convict ship and how her second child born on the ship had died. When she arrived in Botany Bay, she discovered that she was the only educated woman there. The men in charge of the colony listened to her views, and her husband built up a fortune. In 1793, he bought land and started to farm sheep. He built an elegant house and was nicknamed 'hero of the fleece'.

John Macarthur, however, was quarrelsome. Even before he bought the land he fell out with the governor of the colony. In 1809, he joined a rebellion against Governor Bligh and, when it failed, he had to leave Australia. Elizabeth remained, looking after their eight children and running the farm, building up their wool business, and travelling all over Australia selling wool.

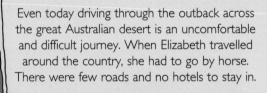

Even today driving through the outback across the great Australian desert is an uncomfortable and difficult journey. When Elizabeth travelled around the country, she had to go by horse. There were few roads and no hotels to stay in.

▼ Sheep were the key to the wealth of Australia. Elizabeth Macarthur established New South Wales as an important wool-producing area.

Lady Hester Stanhope
(1776-1839)

Lady Hester Stanhope was strong willed and witty, and she did not behave the way she was expected to behave. She was the eldest daughter of an English earl. In 1800, she left home to live with her grandmother. Three years later, her uncle, William Pitt, invited her to look after his house and be his companion. Pitt was Prime Minister, and Hester entertained many important people. She was well known for her sharp tongue and quick wit which made her as many enemies as friends. When Pitt died in 1806, the government gave her a pension of £1200 a year. 'Not enough to run a carriage', said Hester in disgust. In 1810, she left England, never to return.

She sailed for the Middle East with two friends. They were shipwrecked off

Lady Hester hated to be alone. Many Europeans visited her in her monastery on Mount Lebanon. She made them stand up for hours at a time, while she talked non-stop, haranguing them with her views, as Arab servants knelt at her feet.

Rhodes, but carried on to Jerusalem. After travelling for three years, Hester eventually settled on the slopes of Mount Lebanon. She always dressed like an Arab man because, she said, the clothes were convenient and splendid. She was one of the first English people to travel among the tribespeople of Egypt and Syria, but she was treated as an equal by Arab rulers. She became more and more interested in astrology and religious beliefs. The local Arabs thought she was like a goddess, but she died alone, neglected and in debt.

Isabella Bird Bishop
(1831-1904)

Isabella Bishop suffered from an illness of the spine and was advised to travel abroad to rest. In fact, she travelled all over the world, showing great courage as she explored dangerous countries, sometimes on her own.

Isabella's maiden name was Bird. She was born in Yorkshire and brought up in a strongly religious family. Because of her illness, she spent a lot of time outside and learned to ride a horse without fear. After an operation on her spine in 1851, Isabella was told to go on a sea voyage to recuperate. She sailed across the Atlantic and spent seven months travelling in Canada and the United States. When she returned to England, she wrote *The Englishwoman in America*.

For the rest of her life, Isabella travelled constantly. She went to Australia, New Zealand, the Sandwich Islands and Japan. In 1881, she married Dr John Bishop, but he died five years later. Isabella continued to travel, but now she linked her expeditions to missionary work. She went to Tibet, India and across the Middle East, setting up hospitals on the way. After every expedition, she wrote articles and books. In 1897, she journeyed in Japan, Korea and travelled 13,000 kilometres right through China on her own. She left behind her three mission hospitals in memory of her husband, her sister and her parents. She died with her trunk packed ready for another expedition.

Isabella Bishop was very emotional and often extreme. 'I do not care for any waterfall but Niagara', she declared. Her books and lectures vividly describe the places she visited. In 1892, she became the first woman to be made a fellow of the Royal Geographical Society.

Freya Stark
(1893-1994)

Freya Stark travelled through Arabia, riding on a mule or a camel, and often on her own except for guides. She lived with local people and wrote about her experiences in articles and books. She became a well-known traveller and expert on the Middle East.

Freya's parents were artists, and her upbringing was not like that of most Victorian children. She was born in Paris and could speak English, French and Italian by the time she was 5 years old. When she was 35, she went to Lebanon and Syria to travel with a friend through the little-known countryside. Freya had already learned Arabic, the language of most of the Middle East. She wrote an article about her adventures and sent it to a magazine in London describing the remote landscape and the people with such energy and enthusiasm that her article was a great success.

She returned again and again to the Middle East, Iraq, Iran and the Yemen. She wrote several books and was given an award by the Royal Geographical Society for her work in surveying the remote district of Luristan in Iran. During World War II she collected information for the government and set up groups of local people to support democracy against the fascism of Italy and Germany. After the war, she continued to travel, write and lecture.

Freya Stark wrote thousands of letters, most of which have been kept. She described her impressions to her friends as she travelled, and kept a copy of each letter so she could use the information later in her books, lectures and articles.

▼ Freya Stark travelled on mules through the Middle East in 1928 with a friend and a local guide.

Amelia Earhart
(1898-1937)

Amelia Earhart was the first woman to fly across the Atlantic, and the first to fly solo across the Atlantic. She showed that women could be as adventurous as men and that flying was fun.

Although Amelia was born in Kansas, her first job was in Canada in 1917, nursing wounded soldiers and airmen from World War I. She was fascinated by the tales of the airmen and took flying lessons from Neta Snook, one of the first women pilots. In 1928, when she was invited to fly across the Atlantic, Amelia leaped at the chance. She did not pilot the plane but still became famous.

Four years later, Amelia made the flight again, this time flying solo. In 1937, she set off on a round-the-world flight with Fred Noonan as navigator. On 2 July, they took off from New Guinea but were never seen again. It is probable that they ran out of fuel and crashed in the ocean.

The first aeroplane was flown by the Wright brothers in 1903, but it was not until World War I that thousands of aircraft were built and used. Even after the war, flying was still risky. There was no radar and aircraft carried few instruments.

◀ Amelia Earhart at the controls of her aircraft. Her solo Atlantic flight took fifteen hours, but all she took with her was a flask of soup.

Amy Johnson
(1903-1941)

Amy Johnson was a famous aviator. She broke several records, flying alone in a small plane thousands of kilometres across the world. People admired her spirit and daring, and the press called her the 'Queen of the Air'.

Amy was born in Hull, England, where her father was a fish merchant. She graduated from university and took a badly paid job as a secretary. Her one aim was to save money and learn to fly. Her parents were not sure that this was a good idea, but they thought that becoming a commercial pilot might be all right. Amy also trained as a mechanic and became the first woman in Britain to get a licence as a ground engineer. In 1928, she gained her pilot's licence. At once, she set her mind to breaking records. Although she had only flown for fifty hours, she persuaded a backer to give her money, and in 1930 she took off for Darwin in Australia. It took seventeen days, and was the first time a

woman had made the flight. She missed the record by three days, but immediately became famous and was able to raise money for her next flight by giving lectures and writing articles. In 1931, Amy made a record flight across Siberia to Tokyo. The next year, she married another pilot, Jim Mollison, and knocked ten days off his record flight to Cape Town in South Africa. After that, they flew together until their marriage broke up in 1938. When World War II broke out, Amy joined the Women's Auxiliary Air Force. She disappeared while flying over the River Thames during bad weather.

When Amy Johnson learned to fly, most pilots were men who had flown planes during World War I. Even today, there are many more male pilots than female.

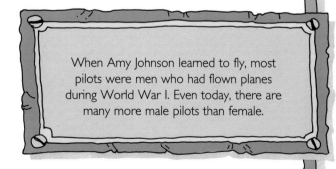

◀ When Amy returned home after her flight to Australia in 1930, she was welcomed warmly.

Sheila Scott

(1927-1988)

Although Amy Johnson (see page 105) was killed during World War II, her pioneering work was continued by Sheila Scott. During the 1960s and 70s, Sheila broke over one hundred aviation records and won over fifty trophies.

She was born Sheila Hopkins in Worcester, England. She left school in 1943, in the middle of World War II, and joined the Voluntary Air Detachment as a nurse. When the war ended, she worked as an actress for a year, getting small parts in films and theatre, and changed her name to Sheila Scott. In 1959, she learned to fly and entered for a race between London and Cardiff. She flew an old RAF biplane, and to her surprise she came fifth. Encouraged, she entered more races. In 1960, she won the De Havilland Trophy. She began to set her sights further afield. In 1965, she flew on her own to cover 50,000 kilometres around the world. It took thirty-three days and 189 hours of flying time. It was the longest solo flight in a single-engined plane. In 1971, she was the first person to fly solo in a light aircraft from equator to equator over the North Pole.

There are no longer air races, or attempts to break air records as Sheila Scott did. In the 1960s and 70s, air travel became much cheaper and very popular. There are now so many planes flying in and out of airports that air races seem an extraordinarily dangerous idea. Space travel has captured the public's imagination instead.

▼ Sheila Scott is interviewed before her 1971 flight. The American space agency, NASA, monitored her physical and mental reactions during the journey.

Valentina Tereshkova
(born 1937)

Valentina Tereshkova was the first woman to travel into space. She was born on a farm in the Russian village of Maslennikovo. She worked in a factory but longed for something more exciting. In 1959, she tried parachute jumping and soon became good at it. Two years later, Yuri Gagarin made the first flight into space. Surely, Valentina thought, she could do that? She wrote to the Russian space authorities and volunteered to become an astronaut. She was ideal. As well as being an expert parachutist, she belonged to the Young Communist League, Comsomol.

For two years, Valentina trained hard. She exercised, practised being weightless and learned the technical skills of space flight. On 16 June, 1963, her spaceship *Vostok VI* was rocketed into space to orbit the Earth. She stayed in space for three days, making forty-eight orbits and travelling over a one and a half million kilometres. The Russian people were proud of her. She was given awards and named Hero of the Soviet Union.

Valentina proved that women astronauts were more than equal to men. The Russian President Khrushchev pointed out that, when she returned to Earth, Valentina had been in space longer than all the male American astronauts put together. Only people in the West, he said, thought that women were the 'weaker sex'.

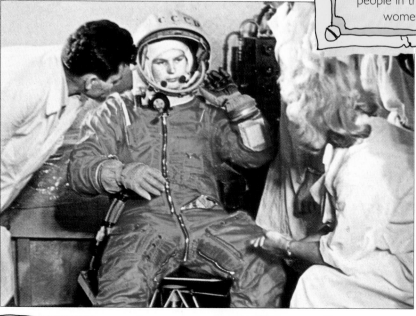

◀ Valentina prepares for her flight. As well as showing that women could be astronauts, Valentina travelled abroad to give lectures and promote friendship between Russia and other nations.

Puzzle

Write the answers to the clues in the boxes, starting each answer at the arrow. Write in the answers to clues 1-9 between the 'start' and 'finish' points outside the circle (clockwise). Write the answers to clues 10-16 between the 'start' and 'finish' points inside the circle (anti-clockwise).

Some of the letters have been filled in for you.

When you have filled in the answers correctly you will see that there are two words around the centre of the circle that describe *fields of human achievement.*

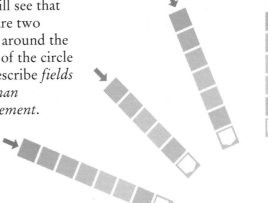
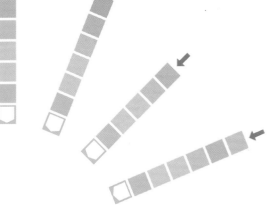

(clue 1)

(clue 10)

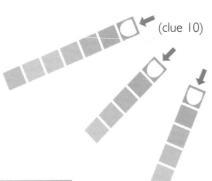
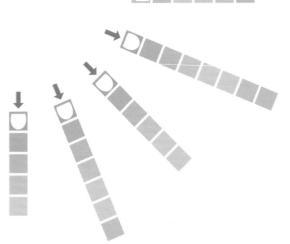

Clues

1 Australian Aboriginal writer and civil rights campaigner (Page 35)
2 She and her daughters fought for women's right to vote (first name) (Page 24)
3 French fashion designer and creator of perfumes (Page 57)
4 Name of gorge in East Africa where Mary Leakey found remains of early hominids (Page 98)
5 Silent ------ is the title of a famous book on ecology by Rachel Carson (Page 96)
6 Japanese author of 11th-century novel, *The Tale of Genji*, Shikibu -------- (Page 61)
7 Rhodesian independence fighter and then government minister in Zimbabwe (Page 52)
8 Black American poet, writer, singer and campaigner (Page 36)
9 First woman winner of the Nobel Peace Prize for founding settlement houses (Page 25)

10 Elizabeth Blackwell founded the Woman's ------- College of New York Infirmary (Page 84)
11 Famous novel about slavery by Harriet Beecher Stowe, ----- *Tom's Cabin* (Page 19)
12 Helen Suzman, Catherine Spence and Mary Wollstonecraft all fought for universal -------- (Pages 34, 22, 17)
13 Daughter of Marie Curie, also a physicist studying radiation (first name) (Page 90)
14 Mother Theresa, Sue Ryder and Cicely Saunders all did this kind of work, which involves freely helping other people (Pages 13, 15, 14)
15 English novelist, author of *Pride and Prejudice* (Page 64)
16 Irish scientist, famous for her work with molecular crystals (Page 94)

Answers can be found on page 111 at the back of the book.

Index

Picture Acknowledgements

The publishers would also like to thank: Metropolitan Museum of Art, New York; British Library, London; Guildhall Library, Corporation of London; Royal Geographical Society, London; Maidstone Museum and Art Gallery, Kent; Kentchurch, Hereford; Walker Art Gallery, Liverpool.

a = above l = left
b = below r = right
AKG: 63a. Ancient Art and Architecure Collection: 39a; 39b. Anne Frank Stichting (© AFF/AFS Amsterdam, The Netherlands: 16a Associated Press: 49a; 49b; 106. Barnabys Picture Library: 35b. Bridgeman Art Library: 10a; 10b; 20b; 37b; 38a; 38b; 40; 42a; 42b; 43a; 44a; 44b; 45a; 45b; 47b; 53a; 53b; 54a; 54b; 62b; 69b; 71b; 74a (© Alan Bowness/Barbara Hepworth Estate); 74b (Peter Kinnear). Camera Press: 52a; 52b (Tudor Lomas). Christian Science Society: 55a; 55b. Cinema Museum, Ronald Grant Archive: 17b; 64b; 72b; 79. E.T. Archive: 8a; 9a; 9b; 43b; 46a; 57a (Roger Schall); 61; 66b; 104a. Mary Evans Picture Library: 18b; 19a; 41a; 56b; 67a; 67b; 85b; 90a; 105b. Robert Harding: 23a; 29a; 32a (FPG International); 63b; 75a (Donald McLeish); 87b (FPG International): 88b (Los Alamos Scientific Laboratory);

90b (Roger Viollet); 91a: 92b (FPG International); 96b (M. Leslie Evans); 100a Ian Sumner; 100b. Hulton Deutsch: 16b; 17a; 24a; 24b; 25a; 26b; 28a; 28b; 32b; 37a; 41b; 47a; 51a (Reuters); 58a; 58b; 62a; 64a; 66a; 69a; 70a; 70b; 71a; 76a; 76b; 78b; 82a; 84; 89b; 94a; 97b; 105a. Hutchison Library: 22b (Bruce Wills); 35a (Andre Singer), Laura Ashley: 59a; 59b. Magnum Photos: 13a (Raghu Rai); 30b (Mark Ribaud); 33a (Dennis Stock); 33b (Dennis Stock); 34a (Ian Berry); 34b (Abbas); 36b (Phillip Jones Griffiths); 50a (Marilyn Silverstone); 50b (Marilyn Silverstone); 51b (Abbas); 75b (Robert Capa); 77b (Gideon Mendel); 80 (David Hurn). Mansell Collection: 8b; 29b; 48a; 48b; 101a; 101b. National Portrait Gallery: 65; 72a. Network: 14a (Laurie Sparham); 57b (Kammerman); 60a (Nike Abrahams); 60b (C. Pillitz); 77a (Fay Godwin). Oxford Picture Library: 81b.

Range Pictures/Bettman: 12a; 13b; 18a; 20a; 21a; 21b; 24a; 25b; 26a; 27a; 27b; 30a; 31a; 31b; 36a; 46b; 56a; 68; 73; 78a; 83; 88a; 92a; 93a; 96a; 104b. Royal Geographical Society: 102; 1031; 103b. Save the Children Archives: 11a; 11b. Science Photo Library: 81a; 82b; 85a; 86. 87a (National Library of Medicine); 89a (Tony Craddock); 91b (David Scharf); 93b (Dr. Jeremy Burgess); 94b (Clive Freeman/ Biosym Technologies; 95a; 95b (David Parker); 97a (Dr. Arthur Lesk, Laboratory for Molecular Biology); 98a (John Reader); 98b (John Reader); 99a (Julian Baum/New Scientists); 99b (François Gohier); 107a (Novosti); 107b (Novosti). Sue Ryder Foundation: 15a; 15b. Syndication International: 19b. *Front cover (clockwise from top left)* E.T. Archive; Bridgeman Art Gallery; Bridgeman Art Gallery; E.T. Archive; E.T. Archive; Range Pictures/Bettman; Science Photo Library (John Reader);

Magnum Photos (Raghu Rai); Bridgeman Art Gallery; Mary Evans Picture Library; Science Photo Library (Novosti); Hulton Deutsch (Reuters). *Back cover (clockwise from top left)* Mary Evans Picture Library; Hulton Deutsch; Network (Mike Abrahams); Bridgeman Art Gallery; Bridgeman Art Gallery; Range Pictures/Bettman; Bridgeman Art Gallery; © Alan Bowness/Hepworth Estate/Peter Kinnear; Mansell Collection; Robert Harding (Marilyn Silverstone); Mansell Collection.

Introduction Bridgeman Art Gallery: 3r; 4a; E.T. Archive: 3l; 3b; Robert Harding (FPG International): 4b

Puzzle (clockwise from top left) Mary Evans Picture Library; Range/Bettman; Camera Press; Magnum Photos (Raghu Rai); Hulton Deutsch; Bridgeman Art Library; E.T. Archive (Roger Schall); Bridgeman Art Library; Hulton Deutsch; Hulton Deutsch